How to Get Your Name in the Dictionary

The Lives Behind Eponyms

Grace Tierney

CONTENTS

Introduction

The English language is a cornucopia, brimming with words to amaze and delight. Flip open a dictionary at any page and you'll find treasure. Since 2009 I've explored extraordinary words weekly on the Wordfoolery blog and in 2013 I began a series of posts exploring eponyms.

An eponym is a person or thing, real or fictional, for which an invention, discovery or object is named. For example Louis Braille is the eponymous inventor of a reading system for those with sight loss.

I discovered the lives behind eponyms are incredibly varied and span centuries and continents. Any history of the English language is also the history of the men and women who gave their names to the dictionary. This book is my tribute to them.

My eponymous heroes and heroines range from sharp-shooting teenage girls to lovers escaping palaces on bed-sheet ropes. Ingenious inventors and daring scientists feature, of course, but so do soldiers, chefs, goddesses, revolutionaries, murderers and their victims, villains galore, and an elephant. These people shaped our language and changed our world.

If you'd like to add your own name to the English dictionary let their stories guide you.

1
Tickle Tastebuds

Food and fame are inextricably linked. Some dishes are named in honour of those we revere, while others are named for their creator or the location of their creation. This is an area where the French language donated generously to English.

One thing is sure though, if you want to get your name into the dictionary, it's time to grab an apron or a cocktail shaker.

Along with the dishes and drinks in this chapter you'll find food science breakthroughs, catering equipment, and one cocktail you'll never want to drink.

Aphrodisiac

An aphrodisiac is a food or drink deemed to stimulate sexual desire. They are named for Aphrodite, the Greek goddess of love and beauty. According to Homer she was born from the sea foam as daughter of Dione and Zeus.

Zeus, fearing the gods would fight over her amazing beauty married her off quickly to Hephaestus, the smith god. He showered her with jewellery and crafted a magical girdle of finely wrought gold for her. Unfortunately it increased her appeal and her infidelity was legendary.

Her festival, Aphrodisiac, was celebrated around Greece. Her priestesses were women who represented the goddess. The Greeks believed intercourse with the priestesses was the best way to worship Aphrodite.

Apples

Many varieties of fruit and vegetables are named for their creators and don't qualify as eponyms. Apples are a notable exception as customers will request them by name. "I'll have six Granny Smiths, please".

The Bramley apple is named for Matthew Bramley. Matthew, a butcher, bought a cottage in Nottinghamshire, England in 1846. The cottage had a bramley apple tree in the garden originally planted by Mary Ann Brailsford in 1809. It's not known where she found it.

Cox's Orange Pippin apples are named for Richard Cox (1776-1845), a retired brewer, who developed the apple in Buckinghamshire, England.

The Granny Smith apple originated as a chance seedling tended by Maria Ana "Granny" Smith in Australia in 1868.

Finally the original apple, according to the Book of Genesis, gives us the eponymous anatomical term Adam's apple.

Bain-marie

A bain-marie is a vessel filled with hot water into which another dish is lowered in order to cook something slowly or to keep it warm. It is used for gently melting chocolate, for example.

This French term translates as the "bath of Mary" and possibly refers to Mary, the mother of Jesus.

Others believe this is a bad translation and bain-marie actually refers to Miriam in the Old Testament, the sister of Moses. Miriam was said to have written a book on alchemy which might explain the equipment link, but there are no bathing references to either Mary or Miriam in the Bible.

Béchamel Sauce

This white sauce made from flour, butter, and milk is flavoured with herbs and vegetables. It is named for the French financier Marquis Louis de Béchamel (1603-1703) who was the honoury chief steward to King Louis the XIV of France.

It is likely the sauce pre-dated his use of it and came from Italy. Béchamel sauce may even have been invented by several different chefs at roughly the same time.

In the 1600s fresh milk was the preserve of the very wealthy, or dairy farmers, so this rather simple sauce was sophisticated in its day. The original sauce recipe was considerably more flamboyant than the modern one. It called for old hens and partridges as ingredients.

Béchamel lived to a hundred years of age, a rare feat at

the time. Perhaps the French aristocrats thought his sauce was the secret to his longevity?

Caesar Salad

Caesar salad has nothing to do with the Roman Emperor of the same name. It was created in 1924 by chef Caesar Cardini, an Italian restauranteur in Tijuana, Mexico. Caesar and his brother ran their business in Mexico to circumvent prohibition laws in the U.S.A..

One day he ran low on ingredients and he created the salad in the centre of the dining room to impress his Hollywood guests. He mixed lettuce, olive oil, croutons, parmeasan, lemon juice, and garlic. Later in his career he bottled the dressing that had taken his name and his version is still available to buy.

Julia Child, the famous American chef and cookbook author, who dined in Caesar's restaurant as a child, remembered him making the salad at her table and later got the recipe from his daughter.

Eggs Benedict

A popular breakfast, eggs benedict consists of a toasted split English muffin topped with poached eggs, grilled bacon or ham, and hollandaise sauce.

One story has it that LeGrand Benedict, a Wall Street financier, complained in the 1920s about the lack of menu choice at Delmoncio's restaurant and the chef concocted the dish for him.

Another story has it that Lionel Benedict, a Wall Street broker, invented it and ordered it at the Waldorf Hotel in 1894. The chef there, Oscar Tschirky, put it on the menu.

The Waldorf claim is earlier and it's tempting to wonder if LeGrand and Lionel were related. The truth may never be decided but in the meantime it's a tasty debate.

Oscar Tschirky, the chef-maître d'hôtel at the Waldorf, is also credited with creating the Waldorf salad. It's a pity he didn't manage to name either dish after himself or he'd be in the dictionary by now.

Epicure

An epicure is one who cultivates discriminating taste in food and wine.

Epicureans are named for Epicurus (341-270 B.C.), a Greek philosopher who instructed his followers to aim for moderation in all things. This doesn't sound like an epicurean concept. How many foodies stop at a small slice of something delicious?

He also believed the highest good is pleasure. Now that ticks more boxes for the modern foodie who should also note that he was almost certainly a vegetarian. He recommended a self-sufficient life surrounded by friends.

Epicurus lived in a turbulent period and philosophy wasn't always a peaceful or safe pursuit. He once had to flee for his life from the island of Lesbos (another eponym).

His school was based in the garden of his home and unusually for his time, he admitted female and slave students to his small circle of followers.

Gimlette

A gimlette is a drink of gin and lime juice.

The naval Surgeon Admiral Sir Thomas Gimlette (1857-1943) concocted this beverage to convince sailors to drink fruit juice and hence avoid scurvy.

It's possible Sir Thomas didn't make this order effective in the navy as it wasn't mentioned in his obituary, but that never stood in the way of a good story. The image of the respected doctor ordering up cocktails as medicine is hard to resist.

Grog

Grog is any diluted spirits, usually rum, given to sailors.

This nautical tipple was named for Old Grog, the nickname of British admiral Sir Edward Vernon (1684-1757). He issued grog rations to the sailors on his ship in 1740 to end drunken brawling on board thanks to the straight rum which was normally issued to the crew. Dilution reduced the drunkeness, but didn't remove alcohol entirely from the ship.

The dilution proportions varied and gained compass-related names. "Due North" was pure rum while "Due West" was water only.

Grog rations failed to eradicate discipline issues and the quantities were tweaked for many years, once even by the wonderfully-named Admiralty's Grog Committee. I'm sure that was a popular posting.

Grog also gives us the word groggy which was originally used to describe a hangover from the excess consumption of grog.

Old Grog, who became a vice admiral at the young age of 24, gained his nickname by wearing a cloak made of grogram during bad weather. Grogram was a coarse fabric made of wool and mohair or silk.

The grog ration was finally eradicated in the Royal Navy in 1970 after the British parliament held the Great Rum Debate.

Joe

Joe is U.S. slang for a cup of coffee.

Joe is named for Josephus Daniels (1862-1948). Josephus was Woodrow Wilson's Secretary of the Navy and abolished the officers' wine mess aboard naval ships in 1914, thus leaving coffee as the strongest drink on board.

Kir

While several people have cocktails named in their honour, not many alcohols are eponyms.

Canon Félix Kir (1876-1968) was a mayor of Dijon (of the eponymous mustard) in France from 1945 to 1968. 23 years as mayor proves his enduring popularity. During World War II he was the leader of the Burgundy region's resistance movement. He was also a priest.

In honour of his heroic deeds the people of Burgundy named a new liquer for him which seems fair as he invented it.

Canon Félix created kir by blending local dry white wine and crème de cassis, a blackcurrant liquer. When combined with champagne the resulting cocktail is called a Kir Royale, so actually he got an alcohol *and* a cocktail named in his honour, lucky man.

It is believed that kir's fame spread thanks to Canon Félix's other hobby – twinning towns in different countries for promoting trade and peace. He served the drink to visiting delegates, and of course it helped disguise any wine quality issues in less than vintage years.

Lush

The origins of the world lush to describe a drunk are lost to history, possibly in an alcohol-induced haze, but this version should be true.

The City of Lushington Club was an actor's drinking club in London. Founded in the mid 18th century, the members met in the Harp Tavern in Great Russell Street until the 1890s.

The name of the club is thought to come from Dr. Thomas Lushington (1590-1661), a chaplain who was a drinking companion of Bishop Richard Corbet. Dr. Lushington was well known to be fond of the drink and his descendents became ale brewers so his name seemed good for a drinking club.

The members of the club were called lushes and by the 1920s the term lush described someone who was habitually drunk.

Macadamia Nuts

Macadamia nuts come from Australia and although they are named for John MacAdam (1827-1865) he didn't discover them or introduce them worldwide.

MacAdam's German-Australian botanist friend Ferdinand Von Mueller (1825-1896) discovered them and named them for him.

Von Mueller sent some to the Botanical Gardens in Brisbane for study. The director told a student to crack some open so they could attempt germination. The student ate a few and declared them to be delicious.

The wise director waited a few days to be sure the student wasn't going to drop dead and then sampled some himself and said it was the finest nut to have ever existed.

MacAdam was a chemist, medical teacher, politician, and cabinet minister born in Scotland but he emigrated to Australia in 1855 where he became a leading member of society.

Von Mueller founded the National Herbarium of Australia and named many Australian plants. He was friends with Charles Darwin despite rejecting his theory of evolution. Several mountains and a glacier are named for him.

Margarita Cocktail

This tequila-based cocktail could have been invented for, or by, any number of Margaritas – dancers, actresses, and sisters-in-law all claim it.

It is likely to be a variation of a popular Prohibition cocktail called the Daisy which is identical to a margarita but features brandy rather than tequila. Margarita is daisy in Spanish.

Margherita Pizza

When is a pizza not a pizza? When it's a flag.

In 1889, according to legend and shortly after the re-unification of Italy, Queen Margherita of Italy was visiting Naples. Chef Raffaele Esposito of Pizzeria Brandy created a pizza for her in the colours of the Italian flag – red tomatoes, white mozzarella, and green basil.

The longer myth explains that the Queen got tired of formal dinners and banquets. She summoned Esposito and commanded him to make three pizzas for her delectation.

She rejected the first (pizza marinara with garlic). She rejected the second (pizza Napoli with anchovies). The third she adored and he named it after her.

This pizza topping probably already existed in Italian cuisine. Any visitor to Italy will notice they love those three ingredients. There are some timing issues with the events in the tale too.

However, it is certain that his version of the tale and the link to the queen gave it permanent popularity on pizza menus worldwide.

Mason Jars and Kilner Jars

These useful home preserving jars are named for their American inventor, John Landis Mason (1832-1902). In 1858 he used his tinsmithing skills to invent a square shouldered jar with a threaded screw-top lid, and rubber-sealed airtight lid.

This was the era before home refrigeration. Preserving fruits and vegetables in jars usually involved a wax seal which if done incorrectly allowed potentially lethal bacteria inside.

Mason's invention changed all this, but unfortunately for him most of the jars were made after his patent expired in 1879 so it never made him rich. He was later accused (but not convicted) of burning down his home for insurance fraud. He died in poverty in a tenement house in New York City in 1902.

On the other side of the Atlantic the Kilner family of glassmakers in Yorkshire created the kilner jar in 1842. A kilner nowadays has a hinged glass lid and rubber seal but back then it looked awfully like a mason jar.

In an episode of BBC's "Who Do You Think You Are?" ancestry programme Jeremy Clarkson, former Top Gear host, discovered he was a great-great-great-great grandson of John Kilner.

In a strange echo of Mason's story, the Kilner company operated for almost a hundred years but ended in bankruptcy. The design and trademark were bought out and the jars are now made in China.

Melba Toast and Peach Melba

Dame Nellie Melba (1861-1931), the Australian soprano, has four dishes named in her honour and they didn't even get her name right.

She was born Helen Porter Mitchell and adopted Melba as a stage-name as a reference to Melbourne, her nearest city. She debuted in Rigoletto in Brussels in 1887 and reigned over the stage of London's Covent Garden for 37 years.

Her personal life was nearly as dramatic as an opera. Her first marriage was to a hell-raising exiled British nobleman. She held on to her son from that relationship after it disintegrated. However when her affair with Phillipe the Duke of Orleans, potential heir to the French throne, became public knowledge she had to hand over her child and didn't see him again until he was an adult.

She struggled constantly with her weight and once ordered dry toast for dinner at the Savoy Hotel, London. Either the chef took pity on her or in a happy accident the toast arrived as very thin, over-toasted bread. The notoriously hard to please singer devoured it and a legend was born.

The dessert, peach melba, was created for her by chef Auguste Escoffier (1846-1935) of the Savoy in her honour. She was worried that too much ice cream might damage her vocal chords so he added the peaches and all was well. Although I can't imagine it helped with her diet.

Auguste also created the lesser known Melba sauce and Melba garniture (a rich stuffed tomato dish) for his favourite customer.

Her voice lives on in various recordings. Her face lives on thanks to $100 Australian dollar banknotes. Her name lives on in recipe books.

Molotov Cocktail

One cocktail you never want to drink is the Molotov.

Soviet statesman Vyacheslav Mikhailovich Molotov (1890-1986) held various posts in the communist party of Russia from 1917. He was prime minister and then foreign minister for nearly forty years which was a tough job with Stalin as his boss.

In 1956 disagreements with Khrushchev led to his dismissal, and in 1962 his expulsion from the party, although he was re-admitted in 1984.

The improvised petrol bomb to which he gave his name was probably invented as early as 1934 but came to notice when thrown by Finns in 1940 against invading Russian tanks during the Winter War.

The Finnish people had already coined the term "Molotov's bread baskets" for the aerial cluster bombs Russia was dropping on their country under the hated

Molotov's propaganda excuse of "airborne humanitarian food deliveries". So when they developed the petrol bomb they decided it was a drink to go with the "bread".

They tempted the tanks through their lines, separated them from their infantry troops, and picked them off at their leisure with small arms and the cocktails. They even had a state-run brewery, Alko, turning out the bombs.

Did the cocktails work? The Finns, who were vastly out-numbered and out-gunned but high on morale and skills, managed to hold out for substantially longer than expected and inflicted a high death toll on their invaders. They had to cede some territory in the eventual peace treaty but they kept their country. That sounds like a win.

Winston Churchill, a man who liked a drink or two himself, commented of Molotov that he was a man of "outstanding ability and cold-blooded ruthlessness". There's no record of Molotov enjoying cocktails.

Pasteurise

Pasteurisation is the destruction of bacteria in milk or other drinks by a special heating process.

As a student Louis Pasteur (1822-1895) wanted to give

up science to be an artist, but his father forced him to continue, a decision to which millions owe their lives.

Louis, the son of a tanner, studied chemistry but was regarded as a mediocre student. He became a teacher and lecturer. In 1854 he became Dean of Science at Lille University.

Studying bacteria, he discovered that certain micro-organisms were responsible for fast fermentation in wine and beer. Heating and then rapidly cooling the liquid would cause fermentation to stop.

In 1865 he saved the silk industry by devising a method to prevent a microbial disease which was attacking silk worm eggs.

Despite being partially paralysed by a stroke in 1868, he worked on and devised methods of immunisation against cholera, TB, and smallpox. He created the first vaccines for anthrax and rabies. He is known as the father of microbiology.

Pavlova

This meringue-based dessert topped with cream and fruit was named in honour of Anna Pavlova (1885-1931) the famous Russian ballerina.

Chefs in Australia and New Zealand have disputed for decades which country created the dish in honour of Pavlova's 1920s tours of the region but recent research suggests neither country can lay claim to the beloved dish as many versions of it existed in Europe and America long before it reached southern shores.

The arguments will probably continue, but in the meantime we get to enjoy a wonderful dessert.

Anna travelled worldwide with the Russian Imperial Ballet. Her career included a stint with Diaghilev's Ballet Russe and from 1914 she toured with her own company.

She was known for her charity work, especially with Russian refugee orphans after World War I. She once completed 37 turns on top of a moving elephant while on tour in China.

On the day after her death her scheduled performance went ahead in old ballet tradition with a single spotlight circling the stage where she should have been.

Praline

In France praline is a confection of nuts (usually almonds) and sugar. The recipe varies in America and Belgium. It was named after César de Choiseul, Count

Plessis-Praslin (1598-1675).

The count was a French field marshal. A field marshal in the French system is an award rather than a military rank, but he was a military commander with an excellent record of victories and later diplomatic work. After his army career, he served as a minister of state under King Louis XIV.

The count's chef first made praline. Originally known as praslin, it became praline over time. One can only assume that the count had a sweet tooth and no nut allergies.

Reuben Sandwich

This sandwich, popular mainly in North America, consists of corned beef, sauerkraut, and Swiss cheese on Russian rye bread. It is unsurprising that such a hodge-podge of ingredients from different ethnic cuisines was created in the American melting pot.

Arnold Reuben (1883-1970) invented it in 1914 in Reuben's restaurant, New York City, for a particularly hungry actress who wolfed it down despite the messy height of the sandwich and insisted they name it after her.

Arnold replied he would call it a reuben sandwich instead and the name stuck.

Salmonella

Salmonella has nothing to do with salmon. It is a family of more than two thousand varieties of rod-shaped bacteria that cause diseases including food poisoning in humans. It is named for American veterinary surgeon Daniel Elmer Salmon (1850-1914) who first identified it. Or did he?

It is highly likely that his research assistant Theobald Smith (1859-1934) discovered the first strain in 1885 and Dr. Salmon got the credit. After all Theobald was a medical research scientist and Daniel was a veterinary pathologist so who was more likely to find a human disease?

Theobald later left Salmon's team and worked as a professor in Harvard and became director of pathology at the Rockefeller Institute for Medical Research.

Daniel, who was orphaned at the age of eight, had a long career for the U.S. government and made a number of large steps forward in animal welfare — putting inspection and quarantine programmes in place.

Salmon initially thought salmonella caused hog cholera. Sadly some strains of the family are now immune to modern antibiotics. Research is ongoing in how to kill it. UV light and heat are both candidate weapons in this fight.

Sandwich

The humble sandwich, a snack of food between bread, is probably the most famous eponym because its origin is a good yarn.

English diplomat John Montagu, 4th Earl of Sandwich, (1718-1792) was a gambling fanatic possibly because he inherited his estate at the age of ten. By 1762 he would refuse to leave the gaming table for up to two days at a time, ordering his valet to bring him food which was invariably cold beef between two slices of bread either because he liked it or the valet couldn't cook.

Some biographers claim the earl was a hard-working victim of malicious gossip and ate his sandwiches at his desk. Either way, he was a sandwich fan.

The dish became known by his name as others began ordering the same thing but it was almost certainly invented much earlier.

The tradition of lamb, nuts, and herbs between two slices of unleavened bread at Passover dates to at least the 1st century B.C., while in the Middle Ages everyone ate from trenchers of bread which acted as open sandwiches, and a handy way to avoid dish-washing.

John was also the First Lord of the Admiralty during a corruption-riddled era. The consequent weakness of the British navy helped the American side in the War of Independence.

The British explorer and cartographer Captain James Cook (1728-1779) honoured Sandwich, his financial sponsor, by naming what is now Hawaii as the Sandwich Islands. The name lasted nearly a hundred years before gradually the current local name was adopted.

Cook named several other islands for Sandwich too as a gesture of thanks for Sandwich's aid in his role as First Lord of the Admiralty.

The Cook Islands, in turn, are named for the captain. As is a crater on the moon.

Stroganoff

Beef Stroganoff is a dish of beef cooked in onions, mushrooms, paprika, and sour cream. The recipe was named for a Russian diplomat in the court of Alexander III, Count Pavel Aleksandrovich Stroganov (1772-1817). His was a wealthy noble family who enjoyed the arts and fine cuisine.

The palace chef, Charles Briére, presented the dish, which probably had been in the family for some t me, in 1891 to a L'Art Culinare competition and won first prize. Legend has it that the count's teeth were poor and it was cooked to spare him discomfort. The count was a big entertainer and the dish gained popularity.

Although many Russians dispute the inclusion of mushrooms, they were in the prize-winning recipe. Variants of the dish emerged worldwide and there is some confusion over the correct side dish to serve with it. Is it rice, egg noodles, potato straws? Perhaps it doesn't matter as the stroganoff is the star.

The Stroganovs lived in Stroganov Palace in St. Petersburg, which is now the State Russian Museum exhibiting art, sculpture and even items that belonged to Peter the Great. Sadly they do not have a museum café so the rich epicurean legacy of the Stroganov Palace has ended.

Tarte Tatin

A tarte tatin is an upside-down apple tart, flipped before serving, of carmelised apple slices on pastry. The recipe was created by a happy accident.

In the late 1800s, two sisters, Stéphanie and Caroline Tatin, ran a hotel in Lamotte-Beuvron in the Loire region catering to hunters and city visitors. Cooking in haste one day they put a dish of apple slices in the oven without pastry for the apple tart, added the pastry later and flipped it to serve.

Contemporary accounts describe the hotel, opposite the train station that brought visitors to the region, as an oasis of fine-dining and the dish as the crowning jewel on the menu.

The fame of the dish spread after the sisters' demise thanks to Maxim's restaurant in Paris and a rather outlandish, and probably fake, tale of recipe-theft.

Louis Vaudable, the long-time owner of Maxim's, used to hunt around Lamotte-Beuvron in his youth and was keen to get the tarte tatin recipe, but all his questions were rebuffed by the kitchen staff.

He got himself hired as a gardener. Three days later he was fired as incapable of planting anything but in the meantime he had "pierced the secrets of the kitchen" and unveiled the sisters' recipe on his own menu as Tarte des Demoiselles Tatin.

Tupperware

Tupperware is the trademark name for a range of airtight plastic containers named for their American inventor Earl Silas Tupper (1907-1983).

Tupper was a failed landscape gardener who then worked for DuPont chemical company designing lightweight bowls, plates, and even World War II gas masks.

He founded the Tupperware Plastics Company in 1938, developed his special seal and had tupperware in stores by 1946.

The unique marketing plan, the first ever use of party selling, wasn't his idea. In 1948 Tupper took a long phone call from Brownie Wise. A talented saleswoman, she talked herself into a job. Together they removed tupperware from stores and sold it via parties in people's homes.

Ten years later Tupper and Wise had a falling out that resulted in her losing her job. Tupper sold the company to Rexall for a tidy profit.

Then aged 51, he divorced his wife, gave up his U.S. citizenship (probably to avoid taxes), and bought an island off the coast of Costa Rica where he lived until his death. He is the only eponymous inventor in this book to end his days on a tropical island paradise, with perfectly-sealed leftovers.

Turkey

There are two theories for the naming of these festive season birds for the country that straddles Europe and Asia, but both tell us something of the importance of trade, and the bird trade in particular.

The English-centred version goes like this. Turkeys were imported to England from North America on ships owned by merchants from the Ottoman Empire. These Turkish merchants lent their country's name to their birds and over time a turkey bird became a turkey and gradually replaced goose as the bird of choice for Christmas dinner in Britain.

The American-centred version goes like this. When Europeans first encountered turkeys in the New World, they thought they were guinea fowl they'd seen imported to Europe under the name turkey coq because the sellers were from Constantinople (modern day Istanbul, Turkey). The North American bird thus became an Indian turkey or turkey fowl and again over time became just a turkey and a centrepiece of Thanksgiving celebrations.

Turkeys also thrived in South America. The Portugese word for turkey is peru which probably gives Peru its name. So first we have the country giving its name to a bird, and then the bird giving its name to another country.

Waldorf Salad

This famous salad of apple, celery, walnuts, and mayonnaise on a bed of lettuce was created at the Waldorf Astoria in 1896, not by the chef but by the Swiss maître d'hôtel, Oscar Tschirky (1866-1950). It was an instant success.

Oscar of the Waldorf, as he was known, was clearly more than a front of house manager as he also reputecly had a hand in another eponymous dish, Eggs Benedict, and in popularising thousand island dressing. He invented the Waldorf salad for the hotel's first ever banquet and included it in his cookbook (modestly entitled "The Cook

Book") published the same year.

The addition of walnuts was a finishing flourish by the famed French chef Escoffier and has stuck since then. The hotel serves 20,000 of the salads each year.

Any Fawlty Towers fans will recall the famous Waldorf salad incident in the eponymous episode. If you've never seen it, find it online, it's well worth a watch. Basil Fawlty, played by John Cleese, was no Oscar of the Waldorf.

Tschirky had a farm in New Paltz, New York, where he hosted picnics for friends, family, and other chefs. It was later purchased by the Philanthropique Society and operated as a retirement home for chefs.

Conclusion

The creators of new drinks and dishes generally have a hand in naming their creations. If they prove tasty enough or popular enough with the general public they run a good chance of getting their name in the dictionary.

You don't even need to be a chef to manage this feat – inventive customers, famous patrons, and the front of house staff have all used food and beverages to find lasting culinary fame.

2
Be Irish

Being Irish myself this category gives me hope that one day I could add a word to the dictionary. There's no doubt that the ancient Greeks and Romans have a head start on the Irish when it comes to language expansion but we're still working on it and those ancient Greeks are dust.

In fairness I should mention that Scotland and France have contributed a large number of eponyms to the English language too, which is pretty surprising in France's case as the last time I checked they spoke French there.

However I love Irish eponyms and the very first eponym I ever heard was Boycott. His story was part of our history lessons as school children. Naturally as I delved into the world of eponyms, I gathered a few more for this chapter.

Aran Sweater

Aran sweaters, sometimes called fisherman sweaters (or aran jumpers in Ireland), are wool sweaters knitted originally in the Aran islands off the Atlantic coast of Ireland. They are known for their complex raised patterns and have been associated with some wonderful legends.

Nowadays the sweaters, sold by the truck oad to tourists, are usually machine-knitted in a soft pale cream shade but originally they were hand-crafted ir darker colours for the fishermen of the islands and the wool would have been unrefined to make it rain resistant.

The sweaters were made from the fleece of the islander's own sheep and each could take 50 hours to create. Up to 24 stitch patterns were used with each woman knitting her own version of the garmen:. White or cream sweaters were made in smaller sizes for youngsters making their Holy Communion.

Early documentaries about island life in the 1930s (long before running water and electricity came to the islands) popularised the island's crafts and with help from the Craft Council of Ireland and early members of the Irish Countrywomen's Association (an organisation similar to the Women's Institute in Britain) islanders began crafting and exporting sweaters in the lighter colour for overseas shoppers.

Each stitch has a meaning associated with life on the island. Cable represents the ropes on the boats, diamond represents hopes for future wealth, honeycomb represents hard work like the bees of the island, and the zig zag stitch represents the cliffs.

Legend has it that each family's sweater pattern was unique and acted as a method of identifying drowned fishermen. This legend is shared with similar sweaters from the Channel Islands, but in the case of Aran it is unlikely. The islanders formed a small community and missing fishermen would have been known by all.

Just as today, expert knitters varied their patterns for the sheer joy of it. Aran weight yarn is named for the islands too and is used in creating the sweaters. It is known as worsted weight in North America.

Beaufort Scale

The Beaufort Scale is a measure of wind speed at sea or on land devised in 1805 by Sir Francis Beaufort (1774-1857) from Navan, County Meath, while he was serving on the *HMS Woolwich*, his first command as captain.

Naval officers made regular weather observations but

unfortunately such observations were subjective and hence unreliable. Evolving the work of others before him, including Daniel Defoe, he created a wind force scale based on easily observable features such as the movement of smoke, tree foliage, and sails. It runs from zero to twelve. Zero is dead calm. Twelve is hurricane or as Francis said "that which no canvas could withstand".

The scale was officially adopted in the 1930s and was first used on the voyage of the *HMS Beagle* which is better known for Charles Darwin's work. In fact Beaufort had a hand in introducing Darwin to the captain of the *Beagle*.

The scale continued to evolve with use and nowadays weather forecasts are more like to give wind speed as miles or kilometres per hour. However general public weather warnings will still use gale, storm, and hurricane – the terms from the Beaufort Scale.

Francis, who went to sea aged 14, was a lifelong learner and friend of Charles Babbage and other scientists of his day. He had a keen interest in accurate nautical charts having been shipwrecked at the age of 15 thanks to a bad chart. His father published a revised map of Ireland in 1792 so map-making ran in the family. When injured in the Napoleonic wars he spent his recuperation time setting up a semaphore link from Dublin to Galway.

His obsession with charts was noted by superiors and he

became official hydrographer to the Royal Navy at the age of 55, a post he held until he was 80. A hydrographer is a cartographer of the seas and some of his charts are still in use today.

His final rank in the navy was Rear Admiral and his name has been given to part of the Arctic Ocean (the Beaufort Sea) and Beaufort Island in the Antarctic.

Boycott

Captain Charles Cunningham Boycott (1832-1897) retired from the British army and became a land agent to manage the Earl of Erne's estate in County Mayo in the west of Ireland. This was common practice at the time when many owners of large estates in Ireland actually lived in England and were absentee landlords. Their tenants disliked this as the landowners didn't witness the difficulties of the farming class and refused to carry out improvement works.

In the autumn of 1880 there had been a bad harvest in the area and the Land League (something like a union for the tenants which was campaigning to have ownership of land transferred to those who worked it) called on Boycott to ask for a rent reduction to help struggling tenant farmers. He refused.

The Land League, inspired by Charles Stewart Parnell's speech on the subject, "sent him to moral coventry". Coventry is an eponym too – check out the Location, Location, Location chapter.

All tenants refused to bring in the harvest or to have any dealings with Captain Boycott. Shops wouldn't serve him. The postman wouldn't deliver his letters. Even the laundress refused his sheets.

Boycott hired fifty farm labourers from County Cavan and County Monaghan but they required a thousand soldiers to protect them. The harvest, worth £500, cost £10,000 to bring in.

The case became notorious and the Boycott family were forced to relocate to England in a hurry. The story was made into a 1947 film starring Stewart Granger.

To this day boycott is used to describe any protest against people, companies, countries or organisations where there's a refusal to deal with them. The word has passed into other European languages – boykott eren in German, for example.

Burke

To burke is a verb meaning to murder without leaving a

mark on the body and it is named for William Burke (1792-1829). Burke was an Irish labourer who moved to Scotland in 1818 and settled in Edinburgh, renting a room from a fellow countryman William Hare.

When one of Hare's renters died while owing him rent the two men took the body to Doctor Robert Knox, an anatomist, who gave them seven pounds and ten shillings for it so he could use it for his anatomy lectures.

Anatomists of the day struggled to source corpses to dissect as most believed the dead would arise in their own bodies on Judgment Day. Having that body pickled in jars would impede such a resurrection. The profession of resurrection man arose from this demand for corpses combined with Scottish law allowing only the corpses of suicides, prisoners, or orphans to be dissected. Although disturbing a grave was illegal, stealing a body was not as it didn't belong to anybody.

Cemeteries of that era often had anti-theft devices such as locked mausoleums (also an eponym, check out the Be a Greek chapter) or heavy slabs on graves to deter grave-robbers. Watchmen manned towers at night. Families constructed iron cages, called mortsafes, around coffins.

Burke and Hare killed 15-30 victims for the cash, suffocating them and leaving no marks so they appeared to be mere grave-robbers rather than serial killers. When they were caught with the body of a missing woman Hare decided to testify against Burke about sixteen murders and was freed. It is likely that both men's wives were accomplices but only Burke's wife was charged. The case against her was not proven so she went free. A mob attacked her as she made her way back to Ireland and her final story is unknown.

Burke hung in 1829 and the publicity around the notorious case gave his name to the act. The word is also sometimes used in the sense of hushing up or stifling news.

In a lovely touch of irony Burke's body was dissected after his hanging and his skeleton is on display at the Edinburgh Medical School's anatomical museum.

Éire, Eireann, and Ireland

Éire (or Eireann) is the Irish Gaelic name for Ireland and it comes from Éiru.

In legend, Ériu was the wife of the Irish king Mac Gréine. Mac Gréine translates from Gaelic as "son of the sun" suggesting he was a demi-god.

Ériu is sometimes described as the matron goddess of Ireland so it's hard to know if she was a real woman or a legendary goddess but the stories tell us that she led the Tuatha Dé Dannan army in battle against the invading Milesians from Galicia in Spain who landed in County Kerry.

Unfortunately her army was defeated and she was mortally wounded.

Amorgen, the leader of the Milesians, tended her in her dying moments and saluted her courage by promising that the land she had given her life for would always bear her name, Ériu. This in turn gave us Éire (still on Irish postage stamps and coinage to this day). This is Éireann in Gaelic or Erin in English.

Sadly this Irish warrior queen/goddess didn't appear in my Irish schoolbooks possibly because she was also believed to be the mistress of the hero Lugh and lover of a Formorian prince called Elatha with whom she had a son.

Whatever the reason, Ériu isn't well known in Ireland. I think she is overdue some appreciation.

Apparently there's an Eriu river in the Brazilian Amazon region which seems fitting as that region has a tradition of strong women.

Garryowen

Although rugby (another eponym, see the Location chapter) is gaining in popularity worldwide Ireland can't claim to have invented the game. However one County Limerick rugby union club founded in 1884 in the village of Garryowen lays claim to a specific rugby tactic – the garryowen kick.

This seemingly random kick shoots the oval ball high in the air in the direction of the opposing team's try line (scoring line) but its purpose is not random.

While the ball is airborne the kicking team can race forward and attempt to catch the ball from the disorganised defensive line and surge forward to score. The original kicker of the garryowen is often the same player who catches the ball.

The term entered the English language in the 1920s thanks to three years of Garryowen club teams using the ploy to its utmost in winning the Senior Cup in 1924-1926.

Rugby balls, thanks to their shape, are neither simple to kick, throw, or catch in a straight line and this means that a garryowen is far from a sure thing in effectiveness but when done right it is a joy to behold, so long as it's your team, of course.

Guinness

Guinness is an Irish dry stout named for its first brewer, Arthur Guinness (1725-1803). Arthur established his brewery at St. James' Gate, Dublin in 1759, signing a 9,000 year lease at £45 per year. His signature is still copied onto every bottle of Guinness sold.

Ten years later Arthur shipped his first casks of stout and the now Diageo-owned brewery is one of the largest worldwide. The brewery tour is always a popular stop on tourist itineraries.

The brewery took the Irish harp as its logo in 1876. It is based on the Brian Boru harp which is now in the Trinity College library, along with the famous Book of Kells. In the Guinness emblem the harp's curved edge is to the right. When the Irish state was founded and they wanted to use the harp emblem for coinage, the harp had to curve to the left instead because a brewery had prior claim.

Arthur and his wife Olivia had 21 children, of whom ten survived to adulthood. Their descendants include missionaries, "It girls", and politicians.

During the 1798 United Irishman rebellion in Ireland, Arthur was accused of spying for the British. His nickname in Dublin is Uncle Arthur.

The Guinness family, thanks to stout sales, didn't lack funds and were famously generous employers. Their many country estates around Ireland have, in some cases, returned to state ownership over time. Examples include Iveagh Gardens, St. Anne's park, Luggala estate (now part of Wicklow Mountains National Park), and Ashford Castle hotel.

Hooligan

A hooligan is a rough, lawless young person and not somebody I want to claim in the name of Ireland but the word does have Irish roots.

Patrick Hooligan was an Irish criminal, possibly from County Limerick, who was active in London during the 1890s. Patrick and his family (whose real name was Houlihan) based themselves at the Lamb and Flag pub in Southwark in south London and they attracted a gang of rowdy followers.

Patrick worked as a bouncer but side-lined as a tough man, mugging victims in the streets and creating plenty of criminal damage. He came to a sad end, condemned to life imprisonment for murdering a policeman. He died in prison.

His name came to be used as a term for a ruffian from the 1890s onwards in cartoons, newspaper reports, comic songs etc. It even turned up in Arthur Conan Doyle's Sherlock Holmes stories.

Limerick

{with thanks to Limerick-born Nell Jenda}

Short nonsense poems called limericks are generally believed to have been named for County Limerick in Ireland.

The word came into English around 1880 and actually post-dates the best known writer of limericks, Edward Lear, whose first "Book of Nonsense" was published in 1845. Lear wrote 212 limericks over his career. Back then the format was different to what we'd recognise as a limerick today with the first line being echoed or amended in the final line as shown in this Lear example:

There was a Young Person of Smyrna

Whose grandmother threatened to burn her;

But she seized on the cat, and said "Granny, burn that!

You incongruous old woman of Smyrna!"

How the five-line limerick in AABBA rhyming scheme, often with a risqué final punch-line, became associated with County Limerick is obscure. Some sources connect it to a parlour game, others to Irish soldiers serving in France, where the first limericks were written, but the famous Irish sense of humour must be at the bottom of it.

The place name Limerick is actually *Luimneach* in Irish, which translates as "bare ground", but limericks have proven to be fertile ground for witty poets during the last two centuries.

Lynch

The Irish origin of this word is somewhat questionable, but I suspect it has Irish roots somewhere, if only because Lynch is a common Irish surname.

Most of us know that to lynch someone is to punish them, typically by hanging, without the benefit of due legal process. The real mystery lies in working out who was the original Lynch.

The Irish claim to the word is based in Galway city. The story goes that in 1493 James Lynch Fitzstephen, the mayor of Galway, strung up his own son from the upstairs window of his house for murdering a young Spanish man over a romantic rivalry. There's even a plaque at the window which you can see in Galway.

It's a dramatic story and a great one for tourists but almost certainly false because the term didn't gain usage for another 300 years. In fact the window with the plaque doesn't even date from the correct period and is no longer in the original Lynch house.

A variation of the story is that the Lynch son embezzled money from his father's merchant business overseas and covered it by throwing a Spaniard overboard on his return trip. A sailor denounced him on his death bed and his father, a local judge, condemned him to death. When the public gathered to prevent the hanging the father took matters into his own hands and hung his son from the house's window.

It's only fair to point out that second version does include a trial, although one wonders how fair it was.

The much more likely source for lynching (although nobody is 100% certain) is an American Quaker Charles Lynch (1736-1796), a planter in Virginia who held an irregular court to imprison loyalist supporters of Britain during the American War of Independence. Charles later got Lynch's Law passed to excuse him from wrong-doing because it was war-time, a clever move.

The controversy around Lynch's Law brought the word into common usage to indicate anything done without due legal process.

Although lynching later came to be associated with racial issues, Charles was known to be colour blind in his judgments.

Inhabitants of Lynchburg, Virginia will already know of their own connection to this tale, the town was founded by Charles' older brother.

Murphy's Law (a.k.a. Sod's Law)

This sarcastic "scientific law" has been in print since the 1950s. It states that if anything can go wrong, it will.

Again the Irish link here is a little tenuous but as Murphy is probably the most common Irish surname ever, I'm claiming some Irish heritage for Captain Murphy even though he was born in the Panama Canal Zone and he worked in the U.S. army.

Having served in the air corps during World War Two in India, China, and Burma, Murphy became an R&D officer in the U.S. Air Force experiments with rocket sleds, and that experience led him to formulate his law. He took it very seriously as a way to remind developers to plan for all eventualities in their designs. He was infuriated that the press, general public, and some of his colleagues liked to treat it lightly.

Captain Murphy also worked on Project Apollo, which landed the first humans on the moon, and the Apache helicopter design later in his career.

His colleagues at the time claimed that they called it Murphy's Law when he used it to explain a test failure as having been caused by incorrect wiring by one of the technicians. This was seen as arrogance on his behalf and lampooned as such. It didn't take long for the snappy slogan to enter air force lingo, and later general usage.

The law spawned many variations. My favourite is Yhprum's Law (murphy spelled backwards) "Anything that can go right, will go right".

Train Stations

The phrase "train stations" is not an eponym and most train stations worldwide are named for their location or main purpose, but the major train stations in Ireland *are* eponymous.

In 1966 Coras Iompair Eireann (commonly known as CIE, the public company responsible for trains and buses nationwide) decided on the 50th anniversary of the Easter Rising to rename 15 major stations to honor those who struggled to achieve nationhood for Ireland. In fact 16 rebels were executed for their parts in the uprising but as two of them had the same surname (Willie Pearse was the younger brother of Padraic Pearse) they share Pearse Station.

That decision took place before I was born, but to me and anybody younger these train stations are no longer known by the cities and towns they serve but by the names of the men who gave their all in the cause of the country's freedom. You don't ask for a ticket to Dublin's south city centre, you ask for Pearse.

Casement – serving Tralee, Co. Kerry

Roger Casement (1864-1916) was a British diplomat, humanitarian activist in Congo and Peru, Irish nationalist, and poet. He solicited German arms and support for the Irish rebellion during World War I but was caught, tried for treason and hung. Casement also has an Irish Air Corps base named for him.

Ceannt – serving Galway, Co. Galway

Éamonn Ceannt (1881-1916), born in Ballymoe, Co. Galway, was passionate about Gaelic culture and music and became increasingly committed to the cause of Irish nationalism. He was one of the seven signatories of the Proclamation of Independence and had 100 men under his command during the Easter Rising. He was court-martialed and executed by firing squad.

Clarke – serving Dundalk, Co. Louth

Thomas James "Tom" Clarke (1858-1916), born in England to Irish parents, was arguably the person most responsible for the 1916 Easter Rising. He also supported the idea of armed revolution and spent 15 years in various British jails earlier in his life for various political/terrorist offences such as trying to blow up London Bridge.

Clarke was the first signatory of the Proclamation of Independence. He was based in the General Post Office (GPO), the headquarters of the Rising and after the surrender he was court-martialed and executed by firing squad.

Colbert – serving Kilkenny, Co. Kilkenny

Cornelius "Con" Colbert (1888-1916) took part in the Easter Rising. When his group surrendered he took command of the men to spare his commanding officer who was a married man. He was executed by firing squad.

Connolly – serving north city centre, Dublin

James Connolly (1868-1916) was born in Scotland to Irish parents. He was a socialist and union leader who was de facto commander-in-chief of the rebels during the Easter Rising despite having been a British soldier earlier in his life.

After their surrender he told the other prisoners "Don't worry. Those of us who signed the proclamation will be shot. The rest of you will be set free."

He was too badly injured to stand for the firing squad and was tied to a chair for his execution. The manner of his death was instrumental in turning the tide of Irish public opinion in favour of the rebels.

Daly – serving Bray, Co. Wicklow

Edward Daly (1891-1916) from Limerick was in charge of

the Four Courts base during the Easter Rising. Aged just 25 he was the youngest man shot in the aftermath of the Rising.

Heuston – serving the south & west of the country

Seán Heuston (1891-1916) commanded 20 volunteers during the Rising. He worked as a railway clerk in Limerick and had worked in the station which now bears his name. He was executed by firing squad.

Kent – serving Cork, Co. Cork

Thomas Kent (1865-1916) missed the Easter Rising due to a last minute communications mistake cancelling orders to the rebels outside the capital city. He and his three brothers (fellow rebels) remained at home. Rebel ringleaders were targeted for round-up in the aftermath of the Rising. When their home was raided the brothers resisted in a four hour gun battle.

Richard Kent was fatally wounded in the gun fight.

William Kent was acquitted of armed rebellion charges.

David Kent was convicted but his death sentence was commuted to five years penal servitude.

Thomas Kent was convicted and executed by firing squad.

MacBride - serving Drogheda, Co. Louth

Major John MacBride (1868-1916) was a veteran of the second Boer War on the South African side and husband of Maud Gonne, much to WB Yeats' disapproval as he viewed Gonne as the love of his life and his muse.

Because MacBride was known to the British he was excluded from secret planning for the Rising but walked into the midst of it by accident, offered his services, and ended up being executed for his part in the Rising.

MacDiarmada – serving Sligo, Co. Sligo

Seán MacDiarmada (1883-1916) was a radical newspaper editor and helped plan the Easter Rising but took little part in the fighting as he walked with a cane thanks to polio in his youth. He signed the Proclamation of the Irish Republic and was executed for his part in the Rising.

MacDonagh – serving Kilkenny, Co. Kilkenny

Thomas MacDonagh (1878-1916) was a teacher, one of

the founders of the teacher's union ASTI, a playwright, and poet who signed the Proclamation and led troops in the Rising. He was executed for his part in the rebellion.

Mallin – serving Dun Laoghaire, Co. Dublin

On the eve of the Easter Rising Michael Mallin (1874-1916) music teacher, former British soldier in India, and father of four young children played the flute in a recital. The next day he commanded a garrison at St. Stephen's Green and the College of Surgeons.

Mallin is sometimes sidelined by history due to his attempt to avoid conviction after the Rising by casting the blame elsewhere rather than accepting martyrdom. His primary concern at the time was the welfare of his young family and pregnant wife.

He was convicted and executed by firing squad.

O'Hanrahan – serving Wexford, Co. Wexford

Michael O'Hanrahan (1877-1916), journalist and novelist from New Ross, Co. Wexford, was second in command to Thomas MacDonagh during the Easter Rising. He was executed by firing squad.

Pearse – serving south city centre, Dublin

Patrick Henry Pearse, a.k.a Pádraic or Pádraig, (1879-1916) was a teacher, barrister, poet, writer, and nationalist. He and his brother Willie were born on the street around the corner from Pearse Station. He only had one appearance in court as a barrister and instead became fascinated by Irish language, culture, and history so he founded a boys' school, teaching through Irish and English which was a radical notion at the time.

During the Rising he was spokesman, reading the proclamation outside the GPO and six days later issuing the surrender orders to all the garrisons. He was the first of the 16 to be executed.

Pearse's name is remembered in nearly 50 streets, roads, and parks around the island of Ireland.

William "Willie" Pearse (1881-1916) was a sculptor and teacher at his brother's school. He supported his brother throughout the Rising, staying by his side at the GPO rebel headquarters. Willie might have avoided his brother's fate but he exaggerated his role at his court martial and was executed by firing squad.

Plunkett – serving Waterford, Co. Waterford

Joseph Mary Plunkett (1887-1916) was a poet, journalist,

and Irish nationalist leader of the Easter Rising. He came from a wealthy background but suffered with ill health throughout his life.

He worked with Casement to secure an arms shipment from Germany, which was intercepted and scuttled by her own captain. Plunkett was a key planner of the Rising and rose from his sickbed to be at the headquarters.

Seven hours before his execution he married his childhood sweetheart Grace Gifford.

Wondering if other countries name their train stations after people, I found an excellent (albeit incomplete) list on Wikipedia. I particularly like that Cairo has a station named for Ramses II. I believed Victoria Station in London was named for Queen Victoria but apparently it is named for Victoria Street, which predictably was named for the queen.

It seems Ireland is unique in the amount of stations named eponymously.

Wellington

The wellington boot, or welly, is also known on the

American side of the Atlantic as a rubber boot, gum boot, or Alaskan sneaker.

The wellington was named after Arthur Wellesley, the first Duke of Wellington who spent his early life between Dublin and County Meath. Known as the Iron Duke, he had an extraordinary career in military and political circles and he wore those famous boots throughout. Wellington served as Prime Minister of Britain 1828-1830 but his opposition to parliamentary reform led to his resignation. He was Commander-in-Chief of the British Army 1827-1828 and 1842-1852.

He asked his shoemaker, Hoby of London, to adapt a standard leather hessian boot to have a low heel and calfskin lining so they could take him from battlefield to dinner. He is pictured in an 1815 portrait wearing them with a dapper tassel at the cuff. Given his popularity after defeating Napoleon at the Battle of Waterloo, it is small wonder that they became the boot of choice for hunting and outdoor wear throughout the land.

Allegedly Wellington originated the phrases "pub ish and be damned" and "if you believe that, you'll believe anything".

The capital of New Zealand is named after him and the wellingtonia – a giant Californian coniferous tree also known as the Big Tree. Beef wellington has nothing to do with him, sadly. It wasn't a dish eaten in the 19th century.

Wellington boots weren't made of rubber until 1853. The change was thanks to the meeting of Hiram Hutchinson and Charles Goodyear. The tyre man used vulcanization (another eponym, see the Be a Greek chapter) for car wheels while Hutchinson moved to France and founded Aigle (Eagle) to make rubber boots. Farmers, previously shod in wooden clogs, loved the idea of dry clean feet at the end of their working day.

Interestingly in Australia the boots are sometimes known as Blucher boots. They are named for one of Wellington's colleagues at Waterloo, clearly a muddy battlefield.

Before Nokia became known for mobile phones their main product was wellingtons.

Conclusion

There you have it, the Irish have given the English language several of its most enduring words. It seemed only fair to help out our nearest neighbours.

3
Get Your Name in the Calendar First

As the calendar is much shorter than the dictionary this is a tall order, but it's a shortcut to the dictionary. All the slots are currently taken but they've changed in the past, so why not now?

Before we get stuck into the days of the week I should probably point out that there hasn't always been seven days in a week. The Babylonians used a seven day week and held the last day of the week as different from the rest, but sometimes had an eight or nine day week to align with lunar cycles.

Then the ancient Romans (during the Republic period) used an eight day week with the eighth day as a shopping day to get supplies for the following week. They didn't name those eight days. They lettered them A-H.

Once Julius Caesar reformed the calendar in 46 B.C. the eight day week began to die in favour of the seven day week but for many years both were used side by side. The final conversion to a seven day format was done by Emperor Constantine in 321 A.D.

The Romans then named the days after their gods, the planets, the sun, and the moon. Since then they've been renamed for Germanic and Norse gods.

Although the seven day week has been firmly established since Constantine, there have been experiments with other formats. From 1793 to 1802 there was a ten day week in the French republic. From 1929-1940 in the U.S.S.R. they used a five day and then a six day week.

Days of the Week

Monday

The first day of the week is named for our nearest celestial neighbour, the moon, in English and in many other languages. This makes sense as early humans would have noticed the waxing of the moon and been able to divide up time by its cycles. There were plenty of sun-focused early religions, it stands to reason that the moon got its share of devotion too.

The word itself has origins in Old English and dates from around 1,000 A.D.

Tuesday

This day's name originates with the Old English Tiwesdaeg. It translates as the day of Tiw (also known as Tyr or Tiu). Tiw was the Anglo-Saxon god of war and the sky.

Latin writers identified Tiw with Mars, their Roman god of war, hence the Latin name for the day, dies martis or day of Mars. French speakers will recognise Mardi in this derivation.

Tiw was right up there with Thor and Odin in the Valhalla days but his stories are less told in modern times.

He was a one-handed god because of his courage. A giant wolf called Fenris was prophesised to kill Odin, the king of the Norse gods. The gods decided to restrain the wolf while he was still growing but every bond they devised Fenris tore through.

The gods asked the dwarves to create the best leash in the world using magic. They called it Gleipnir. It was made from six things; the noise a cat makes walking, the beard of a woman, the roots of a rock, the sinews of a bear, the breath of a fish, and the spittle of a bird.

Not a tasty potion and you'd have to wonder about the Norse women.

Fenris wouldn't allow the gods to bind him with Gleipnir unless one of them stuck their hand into his mouth first. In a challenge with echoes in modern Roman legends of the mouth of truth, Tiw stepped up, put his hand in and promptly lost it, to save Odin.

Harry Potter fans will notice a certain similarity in this tale between Fenris the wily wolf and Fenrir the werewolf.

Wednesday

This day has an Old English source too, Wodendaeg or Woden's Day. Woden is also known as Odin, the Norse god of wisdom, culture, and war.

Odin was the god of heroes. If they died in battle the warriors were brought by the valkyries to Valhalla for eternal feasting. He surrendered his right eye in order to drink from Mimir's fountain of knowledge. He was believed to have created humans and the universe.

The story goes that he hung himself on the world tree, pierced his side with a spear and hung there for nine days and nights seeking knowledge of the world through special runes.

Thursday

Thursday, as many know, is named for Thor, yes the one with the hammer.

Thor was the Norse god of thunder who made the thunder with his chariot. He-goats pulled it across the sky and presumably it had rattling wheels and bad suspension to create the noise of thunderstorms.

Thor also has an element named for him, thorium, discovered in 1828 by Jons Jakob Berzelius (1779-1848). It is a radioactive metallic element resembling aluminium and is used in electronic equipment and as a source of nuclear power. Perhaps Thor's hammer was nuclear-powered?

Friday

Frigg, the Norse goddess of wisdom, is the source for Friday. She was Odin's wife and queen of the gods. She could see the future but tragically despite this gift she couldn't prevent the death of her son Baldir, thanks to Loki's trickery, with a mistletoe staff. But afterwards she banished it always to grow high on other trees. This is why we hang mistletoe at Christmas. It must be kept aloft, away from causing harm.

Friday has a different root in Latin. The Romans called it dies Veneris, day of Venus, and French speakers will recognise that in their name for the day, Vendredi. Venus was a busy goddess. She looked after love, sex, fertility, beauty, victory, and prostitution.

Venus had a loveless and childless marriage to Vulcan, but bore children to many other gods. She was definitely not the goddess of loyalty. She bore Timor (fear), Metus (terror), Concordia (harmony), and the Cupids with Ares, the god of war.

She also mothered children with Hermes the messenger god and Bacchus the god of wine. She had mortal lovers aplenty too, including the famous hunk, Adonis. The first of April was one of her feast days but it's better known now as April Fool's day.

Venus didn't just get a day named in her honour, she also got the evening star, the planet Venus.

Saturday

Saturday, the seventh day of the week in Roman times, was named for Saturn, their god of agriculture.

He was also their god of liberation and time, which seems appropriate for a day of the week. The Norse, who usually had a hand in naming days, had run out of inspiration this far into the week and with typical Viking practicality, named it Lordag – washing day.

Saturn is perhaps best known now for Saturnalia, a seven day feast in the depths of winter celebrated from the 17th to the 25th of December. It was the merriest festival of the Roman year. All work was suspended. Slaves were given freedom to say and do as they liked and presents were exchanged.

The planet Saturn is named in his honour.

Sunday

Sunday, as you might expect, has religious origins but it should be noted that where the week began with a reference to the moon, it appears to end with a reference to the sun, again something early peoples would have used to record the passing of time in their lives.

The Romans called it dies solis, the day of the sun, but with the coming of Christianity to the empire it was renamed Dominica, the day of god. Emperor Constantine, the first Christian ruler of the Roman Empire, decreed in 321 A.D. that dies solis should be a day of rest, but he gave an exception for those working in agriculture so seeds and vines could be planted at the proper time.

In many other languages Sunday translates as "no work day".

Tawdry

Describing something as tawdry condemns it as cheap and showy, but it's actually drawn from a saint's name day on the 17th of October.

The Queen of Northumbria, Audrey (also known as Ethelrida) married at an early age to Prince Tonbert but convinced him to allow her to keep her virginity during their three years of married life. When he died she lived in seclusion on the island of Ely for five years, maintaining her vow of chastity. When she married for a second time, for reasons of state, she hoped to continue her vow but her young husband grew impatient and attempted to bribe the local bishop, Saint Wilfrid of York, to release her from her oath.

Saint Wilfrid refused and instead helped Audrey to escape. She fled south with her husband in pursuit. When she reached the promontory known as Colbert's head, heaven sent a seven-day high-tide to separate the couple. Her husband gave up. Audrey took the veil and founded the great abbey of Ely.

She died in 659 from a large tumour on her neck which she believed was retribution for the vanity of wearing necklaces in her youth.

Saint Audrey became the patron saint of the Ely Island and throughout the middle ages a fair was held there in her honour on the 17th of October, which was noted for its silk scarves and fine jewellery, perhaps as a bizarre reference to the manner of her death.

The scarves were known as St. Audrey's laces. Over time the quality "laces" were replaced by cheap fakes and her name was corrupted to tawdry to indicate poor quality.

Months of the Year

Unlike the modern calendar, the Roman year only had ten named months, with possibly two unnamed months in the dead of the year when nothing much happened agriculturally. The invention of calendars has always been closely linked to farming due to sowing and harvesting times.

January

The first month of the year is named for Janus, the Roman god of beginnings and endings. He's an easy one to spot in Roman carvings as he's depicted as being two-faced. One face reviews the past year while the other looks for new beginnings. It seems appropriate that New Year's resolutions are made in this month.

February

The jury is out on this month's name but either way, it's an eponym. Some claim it for the Etruscan god of the underworld, Februus, while others support the claim of Februa, the Roman festival of purification celebrated in this month. The truth is likely to be a mix of the two but I'm rooting for the Etruscans as the Romans monopolise the calendar already.

March

This one is named for Mars, the Roman god of war. This month marked the start of war season in Roman times and was considered the first month of the year in their calendar.

April

April is named for the Greek goddess of love, Aphrodite. The Romans had a version too, of course, Venus. April is generally the month when Spring romance in nature gets underway in Europe.

May

This month is named for the Roman goddess Maia, or Maiesta, the goddess of spring and fertility, who was the daughter of Faunus and wife of Vulcan. The Old English name for this month was thrimilce because they found you could milk a cow three times a day at this time of the year.

June

The 6th month of the year was named for Juno, the Roman goddess of the moon, women, and marriage whose feast fell in this month. She was the queen of the Roman gods, much like Hera in the Greek pantheon.

July

Julius Caesar (100-44 B.C.) reformed the Roman Calendar (giving us the Julian calendar) in 46 B.C. and in the process modestly renamed the month of Quintilis, the fifth month, to July in his own honour.

Caesar's contributions to the English language are discussed in more detail in the Be a Political Animal chapter.

August

August has been a changeable month in history. It was the sixth month in Roman times and was called sextilis as a result. It had 30 days at this time.

The first Roman Emperor Octavian (63 B.C.-14 A.D.) was the great nephew and adopted son of Julius Caesar. After Caesar's assassination in 44 B.C. Octavian ruled Rome jointly with Mark Anthony and Lepidus. Octavian defeated Mark Anthony in Actium in 31 B.C. to become, two years later, the first official emperor. The Senate later awarded him the title Augustus or venerable for his services to the state.

Augustus Caesar, then completed Caesar's reform of the calendar and renamed sextilis to August in his own honour. His birth month was September but he chose sextilis, as it was when he had made his greatest triumphs and achievements.

August originally had 30 days but Augustus didn't want his month to be shorter than Caesar's so he moved a day from February to August to make them both 31 days in length.

The Remaining Months of the Year

September, October, November, and December are not eponyms. They are named for their position in the Roman year – seventh, eighth, ninth, and tenth.

Conclusion

There are four months still up for naming rights, especially if you rule an empire. There is some precedent for such a move.

Between 2002 and 2008 the months of the year and days of the week were renamed in Turkmenistan. The new names came from key Turkmen national symbols described in a book written by Saparmurat Niyazov, their first president for life. He changed January to his own name and gave April to his mother. Two years after his death the old names, derived from the Persian language, were restored.

It's not easy to get a day or month named in your honour, but it's possible and it will definitely get you into the dictionary.

4

If You Want to Get Ahead, Get a Hat

Hats complete any outfit and for centuries were worn almost without exception so it's no surprise that several are eponyms. Popularising or crafting a spectacular or practical new hat could get you into the dictionary. Take your inspiration from those who've gone before you.

Balaclava

The balaclava is the hat which doubles as a face mask. Balaclavas were used for the first time during the Crimean War (1853-1856). This war, in what is now the Ukraine, was fought between the Russians on one side and an alliance of the British, French, Sardinians, and Ottomans on the other.

In 1854 they fought the Battle of Balaclava and it lent its name to this type of knitted headgear. Balaclava (sometimes spelled Balaklava) was a small town near Sevastopol.

The original balaclavas were all knitted, although modern versions have been made in many different fabrics and styles. The knitted ones were sent out from home and distributed to the British troops to help them withstand the cold climate. This was vital as their official supplies of appropriate shelters and uniform always arrived late.

After the war the hats remained popular and are still in use today for lining motor-cycle helmets, diving, ski-wear, etc. Race-car drivers are required to wear a flame-resistant balaclava during races. Police and military units in many countries wear this hat. Russian protest music group Pussy Riot are known for wearing brightly coloured balaclavas, in part to conceal their identities.

Bowler Hat

This is the rounded, black hat with a neat brim, so closely associated with Britain, and specifically the City of London. You may be familiar with it from the father in "Mary Poppins" or from Rene Magritte's self-portrait "Man in a Bowler Hat".

The hard-working little hat was named for its creators, Thomas and William Bowler, London hatters, in 1849. The design was requested by the Coke family for a close-fitting, low-crowned hat. They didn't need something natty for commuting to the London Stock Exchange, but they did want to protect the heads of their game-keepers on their country estate. Low branches knocked off their top hats when horse-riding.

Legend has it that the first customer tested its suitability in an unusual way. He put his bowler on the floor, stomped on it twice and when satisfied, he paid his twelve shillings and left having made millinery history.

This iconic hat has been adopted in various countries for the most bizarre of reasons. It was the most popular hat in the Wild West (not the Stetson, see below, as you would expect). Bolivian women have been wearing it since its introduction by British railway workers in the 1920s.

A gentleman's outfitters on the German-occupiec island of Jersey during World War II gave their entire stock of the hats to prisoners of war forced to build the underground hospital on the island.

The men of the Niger Delta wear them with walking sticks as the height of fashion and they're popular with the marching members of the Orange Order and Apprentice Boys in Northern Ireland.

The bowler hat is known in Canada and the U.S. as a Derby hat because when it was imported there, it was described as "hats like the British wear at the Derby". The derby in question is an eponymous horse race founded by the 12th Earl of Derby at Epsom Downs in Surrey, England. The same race gives us the name of the Kentucky Derby.

Davy Crockett Hat

A raccoon-skin hat complete with face at the front and tail at the back, typically lined with leather and fabric, is known as a Davy Crockett hat. Wearing these hats became a craze in the 1950s thanks to a television series about Davy Crockett. They even made a white fur version called the Polly Crockett for the girls.

Coonskin hats were worn originally by some native American Indians as a traditional article of clothing. European pioneers in Tennessee, Kentucky, and North Carolina adopted it as a hunting cap in the 18th and 19th centuries. Benjamin Franklin when working as ambassador to France wore his as a symbol of his patriotism.

David "Davy" Crockett (1786-1836) was an American folk hero, frontiersman, soldier, and politician. He was known as the King of the Wild Frontier. Known for his hunting and story-telling, he had an extraordinary life.

In his early years he worked as a cowboy and laboured as an indentured servant to pay his family's debts. Then he took work as a farm labourer and apprentice hatter. Later in life he worked as a scout in the Creek War and in the War of 1812. His role as scout was largely in foraging for food and spotting troop movements rather than fighting.

He worked his way up through local and state politics to eventually represent Tennessee twice in the U.S. House of Representatives. He opposed President Andrew Jackson's "Indian Removal Act" but lost his seat as a result.

When he left politics he decided to explore Texas, in hope of a new start, and became interested in the independence struggle there. He was at the Alamo when it came under attack by the Mexican army. He and the rest of the men defended it in the face of overwhelming odds for a number of days. He died there on the morning of March 6th, 1836, at the age of 49 and his body was cremated by the winning side, along with several un-armed survivors who were killed after the final battle.

The Simpsons portray the fictional founder of their town, Jebediah Springfield, as wearing a Davy Crockett hat.

Dunce's Hat

A dunce is a person who is slow to learn and is associated with wearing a conical hat with Dunce written on it.

Theologian John Duns Scotus (c. 1265-1308) was a member of the Franciscan order whose teaching combined Aristotle's and St. Augustine's doctrines but opposed those of St. Thomas Aquinas. His name included the name of his birth village, Duns, as well as his nationality, Scottish.

John studied at Oxford, taught in Paris, and after becoming a Franciscan priest settled in Cologne. He was nicknamed the Subtle Doctor. He was known as liking conical hats. This was either inspired by wizard hats or his love of such hats inspired the popular image of a wizard's hat. Either way it came to denote a wise man. He believed a conical shape might funnel wisdom and knowledge into the wearer's brain.

His teachings, known as Scotism, were accepted by the Franciscans and were influential in the Middle Ages but by the 16th century his ideas were ridiculed by humanists and reformers who considered his followers (known as dunsmen or Dunses) to be reluctant to accept new ideas. Dunce came first to mean someone who is resistant to new ideas and finally to mean being unable to understand new ideas.

By 1624 a dunce's table is mentioned as being a place in the school where punished children were seated apart from their peers. In Dickens' 1840 novel "The Old Curiosity Shop" the conical hat, adorned with Dunce or just a letter D, was a normal part of schoolroom equipment.

Use of the dunce's cap lasted until the 1950s in America but there's hope for the reclamation of John Duns Scotus' reputation. He was beatified in 1993 by Pope John Paul II for his contributions to theology.

Fedora

A fedora is a soft felt hat with a wide brim, a creased crown, an indented pinch point near the front, and a ribbon trim. It can be made in any colour but most popular are black, grey, and brown. It first appeared as a female hat in 1882.

"Fédora" was a French tragic play by Victorien Sardou (1831-1908). The title role of the Russian Princess Fédora Romanoff was played by the famous French actress Sarah Bernhardt (1844-1923) who was notorious for cross-dressing. She made a triumphant return to the stage in the play and the hat she wore throughout set a fashion trend for women, especially those fighting for women's rights, as well as for male wearers.

After 1924 when Prince Edward of Britain started wearing them, fedoras rapidly replaced bowlers, the flat cap, and top hats as the hat of choice.

Orthodox Jews also adopted a black fedora in the early 20th century as part of their daily attire.

The height of the fedora was in the 1920s and as a result it became associated with Prohibition and gangsters. Several screen legends have added to its story – Humphrey Bogart, Frank Sinatra, and Indiana Jones have all helped it along. In more recent times it has been sported by Michael Jackson, Johnny Depp, and the author Terry Pratchett.

Panama Hat

Panama hats are not from Panama.

They are, in fact, from Ecuador, about 700 miles away. So why does everyone think they are from Panama?

The builders of the Panama canal (which really *is* in Panama, in case you're worried) wore these elegant woven hats from Ecuador to protect themselves from the harsh glare of the tropical sun and so inadvertently christened them panama hats.

Alternatively, the hats were exported via Panama in the 19th century and had acquired the name in 1834, long before the canal building commenced. You decide.

The Incas were the first to weave hats from the paja toquilla plant from the Ecuadorean coast. By the 18th century, the hats had made their way to the U.S.. In 1855 a Frenchman living in Ecuador brought some to the World Exposition in Paris and presented one to Napoleon III, a great dandy. In the 1898 Spanish-American War the U.S. government ordered 50,000 of them for their troops in the Caribbean.

In 1906 President Theodore Roosevelt was photographed wearing one while viewing the construction of the Panama canal.

The story of the traditional black ribbon band is historic too. It was added to the hat as a sign of mourning for Queen Victoria in 1901.

The best Panama hats pass an interesting test of quality – they hold water and when rolled up can pass through a wedding ring.

As for Panama, they may not have the hats, but at least they still have the eponymous canal.

Stetson

John Batterson Stetson (1830-1906) was originally from New Jersey on the east coast of America but he went west for his health. A hatter by trade, trained by his father who was a master hatter, he created a hat for himself from beaver fur to wear while panning for gold in Colorado. He wore it initially as a joke but realised the high crown provided more warmth and the wide brim protected him from the elements.

Returning east in 1865 he settled in Philadelphia and with $100 he rented a small room, bought the tools he needed, and ten dollars' worth of fur. A year later he launched his iconic western-style cowboy hat.

Soon it gained the nickname "ten gallon hat" possibly because of an advertisement showing a cowboy watering his horse using his hat.

They were so popular that he became the largest manufacturer of hats in the world. His company is still going in Garland, Texas and as they say "Stetson, it's not just a hat, it's *the* hat".

It is said that George Custer rode into the Battle of Little Big Horn wearing a stetson.

Trilby

A soft felt, narrow-brimmed hat with an indented crown is a trilby. Usually the brim tilts down at the front and is turned up at the back. Traditionally it is made from rabbit's hair felt.

It gets its name from the dramatised version of "Trilby" a hugely popular novel published in 1894 by George du Maurier (1834-1896). The novel was first published in serial form in 1894 in "Harper's New Monthly Magazine". It's set in 1850s Paris and draws on his experiences there as an artist.

In the London stage version of the novel the heroine, Trilby O'Ferrall, wore such a hat. Her character is a half-Irish girl working as model and laundress in Paris. All the male leads are in love with her. She is mentored by a sinister character called Svengali – a name which has since also entered the dictionary. The story is said to have inspired Gaston Leroux's "Phantom of the Opera".

The popularity of the hat soared until the 1960s when the lower head clearance in motor-cars resulted in fewer hats being worn.

George du Maurier, or to give him his full name – George Louis Palmella Busson du Maurier - was Daphne du Maurier's grandfather and also grandfather to the five Davis boys who inspired J.M. Barrie's "Peter Pan".

George was brought up to believe his own grandparents were French aristocrats who fled the French Revolution, but actually they were tradespeople who fled fraud charges and later changed their name.

After studying art in Paris and losing his sight in one eye, he became a cartoonist for British satirical magazine "Punch" amongst others, but as his sight continued to deteriorate he turned to writing. "Trilby" was his second novel and was a bestseller.

The city of Trilby in Florida is named after the heroine of the novel, not the hat.

Conclusion

You don't have to be a milliner to sneak your hat, and name, into the dictionary but it might help. A new design to revive hat-wearing could give you English language fame. Just remember it must fit inside a motor-car.

5
Invent Something

It's not easy to invent the next big thing, a quick look in the patents office will make that clear, but success in this area gives you naming rights. If your invention prospers, it will fly your name into the dictionary.

Algorithm

Algorithms were invented by the 9th century Persian mathematician Mohammed Ibn Musa al-Khuwarizmi. It may not look like his name but the Latin version of his name was Algoritmi.

He was a mathematician, geographer, and astronomer. He introduced the Indian decimal system to the western world. He is considered one of the fathers of algebra. He pioneered the use of zero in mathematics.

The word algebra is drawn from al-jabr – one of two operations he used to solve quadratic equations. His name in Spanish and Portuguese means digit.

After the Muslim conquest of Persia, Baghdad became the centre of scientific study and trade. Mohammed Ibn travelled there and worked as a scholar in the wonderfully-named House of Wisdom studying Greek and Sanskrit manuscripts. He wrote about making and using astrolabes and sundials. He supervised a project to map the entire known world for the Caliph, overseeing 70 geographers.

Apgar Score

The apgar score was invented by Virginia Apgar (1909-1974) in 1952. She was an American pediatrician who as a young anesthetist saved many newborns with earlier interventions as a result of this scoring system for a newborn's adjustment to life outside the womb.

Apgar wanted to be doctor from a young age and with the help of several scholarships became the first female full professor at Columbia University College of Physicians and Surgeons. She specialised in anesthesia at a time when it was barely respected and the pay was low.

When she studied the effects of anesthesia on mothers in labour she made her greatest contribution to the field – a standard method to assess the newborn on heart rate, respiratory effort, muscle tone, reflex response, and colour. After some resistance, the scoring system was adopted for use at one minute after birth and again at five minutes.

In 1959, while on sabbatical, she earned her masters in public health from John Hopkins and devoted the rest of her career to prevention of birth defects through public education and research fundraising. She received many honours for her work.

Despite breaking into many areas previously seen as male-only in an era long before feminism, she maintained that "women are liberated from the time they leave the womb".

Not content with a hectic scientific career she also learned how to make musical instruments. She was a talented chamber quartet musician. She was an enthusiastic fly-fisherwoman and was learning how to fly a plane with the aim of flying under the George Washington bridge in New York.

Bic & Biro

Bic, like biro, is a trademark used to describe a ballpoint pen. It is a shortened version of the surname of Marcel Bich (1914-1994) the French co-founder, with Edouard Buffard, of the Bic Corporation which began existence making parts for fountain pens and mechanical pencils. Bich introduced the ballpoint pen in 1949.

Biro is a trademark used to describe a particular type of ballpoint pen and is named for its Hungarian inventor László Jozsef Biró (1900-1985). He patented his pen, containing quick-drying ink, in 1938 in Hungary but the rise of Nazism saw him relocate to Argentina. His pen proved popular. RAF pilots found it worked better at high altitudes than fountain pens. Towards the end of World War II he found an English company to back his invention but it was soon taken over by the Bic Corporation. Now in France a ballpoint is called a bic, but in the U.K. it's a biro.

Big Ben

The iconic clock tower at the British houses of parliament is on many sightseeing lists and it has a fascinating history. It isn't the tower that's called Big Ben though, it's the largest bell inside it.

In 1834 the Palace of Westminster was destroyed by fire. There were so many spectators of the conflagration that they hampered the efforts of fire-fighters. The only surviving structure was Westminster Hall so a competition was held to design a new parliament building.

The winner, Charles Berry, who legend has it watched the old parliament burn (hopefully without matches in his back pocket), didn't include a clock tower but he was asked to add one. He did, a large one with four faces and a huge bell.

Berry pointed out that he was no clock-maker so the

Astronomer Royal, George Airy, drew up a list of requirements. His insistence that the clock must be particularly accurate angered the clockmakers of the day (accuracy wasn't an easy job) and they declared his specifications impossible.

The only man brave enough to attempt the impossible was Edmund Beckett Denison, a somewhat cantankerous lawyer who made clocks as a hobby. He worked with Edward Dent, a professional clockmaker, to create a double-three-legged gravity escapement to achieve that accuracy.

Meanwhile Warners of Cripplegate began casting the one large bell and four smaller bells to create the distinctive Westminster chime (based on Handel's "Messiah"). The largest bell arrived by barge up the River Thames and then a carriage drawn by 16 white horses. This bell was meant to be called Victoria, for the queen, but the public nicknamed it Big Ben and the name stuck.

The Ben they named it for was either a bare-knuckle fighter called Ben Caunt, or the Commissioner of Works on the new Palace of Westminster, Sir Benjamin Hall.

Then in October 1857, during bell tests, Big Ben cracked - disaster! The bell was broken up, and re-cast in a slightly smaller shape.

When the tower was finished and they tried to hang the new Big Ben, it didn't fit inside the tower. Fortunately when turned on its side and hauled up by a team of men over 30 hours, it did fit.

In July 1859 the clock and the bells began working. However in October Big Ben cracked, again. This time the clock had been installed below the bells so they couldn't easily remove it for re-casting.

Fingers were pointed in all directions until George Airy, the Astronomer Royal, suggested they give the bell a quarter turn, and that's what they did. The crack is still there, chiming away the reigns of six monarchs and 25 prime ministers to date.

Big Bertha

Big Bertha is a translation from German of Dicke Bertha (fat Bertha) which was a reference to Bertha Krupp von Bohlen und Halback (1886-1957), the heiress and owner of the Krupps armaments factory at Essen, Germany where the guns were forged.

The Big Bertha gun was nicknamed by German soldiers after one destroyed Fort Loncin at the siege of Liège in Belgium in 1914. A total of twelve were made in great secrecy by Krupp's factory in the years before the war, as referenced in a recent Sherlock Holmes movie. They were the largest mobile artillery pieces in use by any army and could fire up to six miles. They operated in pairs and each gun had a crew of 240 men to service her. The team disassembled the guns to move them. Re-assembly took six hours.

Despite their strength, the berthas were superior for only two years. They failed in the Battle of Verdun in 1916 to penetrate the more modern reinforced concrete French forts of Douaumont and Vaux.

Sometimes the Big Bertha is listed as the gun which pounded Paris in World War One but in fact the proper name for those guns is a Paris gun. They could fire an impressive 75 miles.

Apparently the fat/big reference was to power and had nothing to do with the physique of Bertha Krupp. It was unthinkable in 1907, when she inherited the huge Krupp's empire for a woman to run the show so the German king, Kaiser Wilhelm II, personally sought out a suitable husband for Bertha. She married his choice, diplomat Gustav von Bohlen und Halbach. He ran the factories and she had eight children, two of whom died in World War II.

When her husband suffered a stroke during World War II, Hitler issued a decree to pass ownership to her son so their war efforts could continue. Gustav was later tried for war crimes but was too ill to stand trial. Her son served five years for the company's use of concentration camp labour, especially at the factory named in Bertha's honour. Afterwards, he restored the company to its major position in the German economy, minus the armaments this time. The last Krupp died in 1986 just under 400 years from the arrival of the first Krupp in Essen, Germany.

Black Maria

A black maria is a police van for transporting suspects and prisoners.

The black maria is traditionally linked to Maria Lee, a strong African American woman who kept a sailors' boarding house in Boston in the early 1800s. She was known for the help she gave police and the expression "send for the black Maria" became linked with the removal of the drunk and disorderly from the streets of the city. When the first horse-drawn police vans were introduced in 1830s Britain they may have been named for this formidable lady.

Sadly there is no reason to believe this tale. The phrase first appeared in print in 1835 and appeared in New York rather than Boston which is odd. An earlier reference was a racehorse called Black Maria in Harlem in 1826 whose exploits were widely reported. Perhaps the swift police vans were named for the horse? Or perhaps the horse was named for the feisty Maria Lee, who knows?

Black marias also exist in Finland although their police vans were never black. The same phrase is used in Iceland, Norway, Serbia, and Croatia. So one thing is certain, its use is widespread and if a large lady called Maria attempts to arrest you, you probably shouldn't resist.

Bobby & Peeler

Sir Robert Peel (1788-1850) founded the Irish constabulary in 1814 during his time as Chief Secretary of Ireland and they became nicknamed "the peelers" in his honour. Then in 1829 as Home Secretary he passed the Metropolitan Police Act and bobby became the nickname for the London police force.

Peel twice served as British Prime Minister and is regarded as the father of modern British policing and one of the founders of the Conservative Party.

From a wealthy family he earned a double first at Oxford and entered politics under the mentorship of his father and the Duke of Wellington (see the Be Irish chapter).

During the first year of the Great Famine in Ireland in 1845 (it should be noted that there were many famines in Irish history) he was Prime Minister. He shipped Indian corn to various points in the country to be sold for a cheap price. This became known as Peel's brimstone because it didn't reach the worst-affected areas thanks to bad roads, the truly poor couldn't afford it, and most hadn't a clue how to cook it.

He also created work schemes where the starving were paid to build roads and he founded relief committees to fundraise from the wealthy to help the poor. His efforts helped to prevent the worst of the famine that year.

Peel, much to the outrage of his own party, managed to garner enough votes in the House of Parliament to repeal the Corn Laws (a price-protection law for domestically produced corn and other cereals) in order to improve food supplies to Ireland and to prevent further civil unease in England.

His Irish friend the Duke of Wellington persuaded the House of Lords to pass the law too. Peel was forced to resign as Prime Minister in the aftermath of the vote.

As a result when the potato crop failed again in 1846 Peel was no longer Prime Minister. Famine conditions were worse as families had used all their slender resources surviving the first year. The new Prime Minister, Lord John Russell, took a laissez-faire approach and presumed those already weakened by hunger could work their way out of their problems in his state-sponsored building schemes.

The five year famine ended in 1850 with a death toll of one million. One in eight died. From 1845-1850 about one and a half million Irish left Ireland.

Bowie Knife

A bowie knife is a stout hunting knife with a long one-edged blade curving to a point. The knife was associated with James "Jim" Bowie (1799-1836), an American soldier and adventurer.

The knife was probably designed by his brother Rezin Pleasant Bowie (1793-1841). Jim gave a carved wooden model of the knife to Arkansas blacksmith James Black to produce it for him. Black crafted one exactly as per the model and a second with a sharpened edge on the curved top edge of the blade. Bowie chose the modified design and a knife legend was born.

Bowie killed six men and wounded 15 others at a duel in Natchez, Mississippi in 1827. In 1831 he was involved in a knife fight in Texas with three men hired to kill him. He dispatched all three with his knife; almost decapitating one, disemboweling the second, and splitting open the skull of the third. The knife's fame was assured and Jim Bowie became a folk legend.

Bowie became a colonel in the Texan army in the war of independence from Mexico. In 1836 fewer than 200 Texans, including Davy Crockett (see the Hat chapter) and Bowie, held out against 2,000 Mexicans for 13 days at the Alamo but they were eventually all slaughtered, including Bowie on his sickbed.

The knife-smith, Black, built a booming business in the knives, refining his skills as he went. He did all his work behind a leather curtain and some claimed he had discovered the secret to making fabled Damascus steel. In 1839 he was nearly blinded by an attacker and had to give up his work. In 1870, at the age of 70, he tried to pass on the secrets of his trade to the son of the family that had cared for him but he'd been retired for too long and couldn't remember his own secrets.

David Bowie, the music legend, took the surname Bowie for his stage name from the knife because in his words "it cuts both ways".

Braille

Braille is the alphabet of raised dot characters used by those with severe vision impairment.

Braille was only partly invented by Louis Braille (1809-1852). In 1819 a French artillery officer, Captain Charles Barbier de la Sierra devised a code of embossed dots and dashes to be read at night and hence avoid enemy fire at lanterns and those using them. It wasn't a success.

Two years later Louis Braille, blind since a childhood accident and then studying, age 12, at the Royal Institute for Blind Youth in Paris, encountered Barbier's system, either via a newspaper report read to him or via a visit from Barbier himself.

Braille dedicated himself to stream-lining the system for use by the blind and three years later, when he was just 15 years old, he had completed the system.

Later he would publish adaptations for musical notation and other uses but sadly his system wasn't taught at the Institute, where he became a professor, during his lifetime. It was adopted two years after his death and is now used worldwide.

Buddhism

The founder of Buddhism was the Hindu Prince Gautama Sidharta (563-483 B.C. approximately). His protective father raised him in seclusion. At the age of 16 he married his cousin, who later bore him a son.

In his late twenties he became dissatisfied with their life of luxury after venturing out amongst the people and witnessing their hardships. He left his young family to seek the answers to human existence and suffering.

Six years of asceticism followed, which convinced him this was not the way. So, avoiding extremes of both luxury and poverty, he tried mediation and a balance in all things which he called The Middle Way.

He is traditionally held to have achieved enlightenment while meditating under a fig tree in the village of Buddh Gaya in Bihar, north east India.

He then took the title Buddha which means the Enlightened One in Sanskrit. He devoted the next 45 years of his life to teaching the principles of enlightenment.

Bunsen Burner

A bunsen burner is the gas burner with an adjustable air valve which is widely used in chemistry labs. This tool is named for German chemist Robert Wilhelm Bunsen (1811-1899) who is credited with its design, although some point out similar designs made earlier by Michael Faraday and others. However it was Bunsen who popularised it.

Bunsen is also famous for his discovery with German physicist Gustav Robert Kirchoff (1824-1887) of two elements – cesium (Cs) and rubidium (Rb) in 1860.

He was one of the most popular scientists of his time, devoted to his students, refusing to take out any patents as a matter of principle, and working quietly to enrich scientific knowledge without engaging in theoretical disputes.

In cricket a "bunsen burner" is rhyming slang for a turner – a pitch that favours the spin bowler.

Crapper

Thomas Crapper (1836-1910) was a plumbing expert and inventor but he didn't invent the water closet or W.C., it evolved over time. The first flushing toilet was invented in 1592 and one was given to Queen Elizabeth I of Britain but they didn't gain traction with the general public until the 1700s.

Crapper *did* innovate several improvements to the W.C.. He also invented the bathroom showroom for the Victorian world, was plumber to Queen Victoria, and ran a very successful W.C. business.

As for the word crap, well he can't claim that either. Crap was an ancient word for chaff, or rubbish, which had fallen out of use in English by the 16th century. However early English settlers of America took the word with them and it remained alive there although it was seen as rather vulgar.

In 1917 American servicemen stationed in England found it hugely amusing to see "Crapper" emblazoned on toilet bowls and began using the word crapper for the entire apparatus. Their English comrades couldn't see the joke.

The name travelled back to the U.S. and stuck fast. Thanks to TV and movies, the term is understood on both sides of the Atlantic now.

Lavare means wash in Latin. This gave us lavatory – a wash hand basin. So many people said they were going to "wash their hands" that now lavatory is seen as the correct term for a W.C..

Cyrillic Alphabet

The Cyrillic alphabet is used for writing Slavic languages such as Russian and Bulgarian. It is traditionally believed that this alphabet was developed by two brothers, St. Cyril (826-869) and St. Methodius (815-885), during the translation of the bible and liturgy into Slavonic.

Cyrillic is composed of the Greek alphabet supplemented with Hebrew letters for non-Greek sounds. It has, of course, evolved over time to reflect the evolution of the Slavic languages.

The saintly brothers share a joint feast day on the 7th of July. They are known as the Apostles to the Slavs. They are patron saints of Europe (with Benedict of Nursia). Both brothers were monks but lived anything but secluded lives, instead working as professors, diplomats, and missionaries across several countries, picking up the languages as they went.

Daguerreotype

Louis-Jacques-Mandé Daguerre (1789-1851) was a French artist, photographer, inventor of the daguerreotype, and developer of the diorama theatre. He is known as one of the fathers of photography.

Trained as a theatre designer and artist, he became a celebrated theatre designer in Paris. Partnering with Nicéphore Niépce, the inventor who produced the world's first heliograph (an early form of photograph) in 1822 and the earliest surviving photographic camera, Daguerre worked on a process which would later bear his name.

After Niépce died, he continued the work and revealed it at the French Academy of Sciences in 1839. He sold it to the French government in return for a pension for himself and Niépce's son and later that year the full instructions were released for all to use as France's gift to the world.

Daguerreotypes were the most popular form of photography for the next twenty years until they were superseded by simpler processes. When viewing a daguerreotype image the object represented appears to float above the sheet.

Daguerre's name is one of 72 inscribed on the Eiffel

Tower. The names are on the sides of the tower under the first balcony and are of 72 male French scientists, engineers, and mathematicians in recognition of their contributions. Sadly the list excludes Sophie Germain, a noted French mathematician whose work on the theory of elasticity was used in the construction of the Eiffel Tower.

Davy Lamp

Coal mines are challenging work environments today but in the past they were treacherous. Seams of coal underground also contain gases like methane and carbon monoxide which when combined become firedamp which is highly flammable.

In the 1800s miners relied on oil lamps while mining and explosions were frequent. On the 25th of May 1812 an explosion in the Felling Mine in England killed 92 miners. Sir Humphry Davy (1778-1829), Britain's leading chemist, resolved to devise a safer lantern and save lives.

By 1816 he'd created the davy lamp. It has the flame enclosed in metal gauze to lessen the chance of explosion. The firedamp passes through the mesh but burns up and the mesh stops the flame from spreading.

However it limits the amount of light emitted by the lamp. George Stephenson devised another lantern where the flame was covered in glass and this became known as the Geordie Lamp.

Both were used and eventually evolved into one lamp. Electric torches replaced both with time. Modern safety laws require ventilation in mines and chemical sensors are used to detect firedamp in the tunnels.

Paradoxically the lamp led to more accidents as areas of mines previously deemed unsafe were then open for exploitation using the lamps but if even one wire of the mesh was damaged, the lamp was dangerous again.

One use of the davy lamp technology remains however. As the mesh protects the flame, it can never go out if it has sufficient fuel. The Olympic torch, the ore (plus backups) that travels from Greece to the site of the games, is a davy lamp.

Davy tinkered with chemical experiments, much to his family's dismay, from an early age. He's also known for isolating the elements potassium, sodium, calcium, strontium, barium, boron, and magnesium. He discovered the elemental nature of chlorine and iodine. He invented an early form of the incandescent light-bulb. Michael Faraday worked for him as a valet and lab assistant. Davy once claimed that Faraday was his greatest discovery.

Derrick

A derrick is a single spar lifting-hoist commonly used to move cargo from ship to quayside or vice versa. The derrick takes its name from Thomas Derrick, an Elizabethan executioner who created a derrick-style gallows for his work.

Thomas Derrick was found guilty of outraging women during the 1596 raid on Cadiz in Spain known as the Sack of Cadiz. He was sentenced to be flogged around the fleet, a sentence which was often fatal.

A sailor sentenced to this punishment was rowed between all the ships in the fleet so sailors could witness his flogging. The sentence could take months or even years to complete. After each flogging was completed his back would be washed with sea water in a vain attempt to arrest infections which gave rise to the expression rubbing salt into a wound.

To avoid his fate Derrick agreed to inflict the same punishment on his fellow convicts and to become executioner at Tyburn. He was pardoned by Robert Devereux, the 2nd Earl of Essex whom he later executed in 1601 for treason, using an axe this time, at Tyburn in London. It took him three strokes with the axe.

Derrick devised a beam with a lift and pulleys for his role as hangman rather than the traditional rope over a beam method. The similarity of this to basic cranes helped name them derricks.

He executed 3,000 people during his career.

Dewey Decimal System

This system of library classification was first published in 1876 by Melvil Dewey (1851-1931) and is now used in 135 countries worldwide. He devised the system while working at Amherst College library.

Melvil supported the idea of spelling standardisation, or as he would say "simpler spelin". He changed his name from Melville to Melvil and even tried Dui as a surname for a while. He was instrumental in organising the 1932 Winter Olympics at Lake Placid.

His main flaw was an "inability to control himself around women". He was rumoured to ask female applicants to his School of Library Economy for their bust size and photograph with their applications because you can't "polish a pumpkin". The bust part is untrue, merc fully.

Diesel Engine

Rudolf Christian Karl Diesel (1858-1913) was a German inventor and engineer best known for creating the diesel engine. Born in Paris to Bavarian parents, he lived in France and London before moving back to Germany for his education.

He excelled throughout his education and gained many patents for the refrigeration company Linde but then moved on to steam engine experiments. One of these exploded and nearly killed him. He then experimented with combustion engines. It was around this time Karl Benz was granted a patent for the first motor car in 1886.

Diesel's interest lay in improving the efficiency of such engines as 90% of the energy in the fuel was wasted. He created the compression-ignition engine to resolve this issue.

In 1900 he ran his engine on vegetable oil without any modification.

His death in 1913 has been subject of many conspiracy theories. He was travelling by steamboat from Antwerp to London when he disappeared. It is thought he committed suicide as after his death a body was found but not formally identified. He had left his wife a bag full of money that would be worth a million U.S. dollars today.

Ferris

Ferris wheels were invented by George Washington Gale Ferris Junior (1859-1896) for the World's Columbian Exposition in Chicago in 1893. His aim was to create a structure that would "out-eiffel" the Eiffel Tower and in that he succeeded because the wheel carried 2.5 million passengers before its demolition in 1906.

Sadly Ferris spent two years in the courts after the fair trying to claim profits he felt were owed to him and he died a year later. Even his ashes lay unclaimed for nearly a year. An unloved and sad end for a talented engineer who was born on St. Valentine's Day.

Ironically the French paid him a huge compliment by erecting a replica of his wheel for the Paris Exposition in 1900. He received the honour of a Google Doodle on his 154th birthday.

Fibonacci Sequence

The fibonacci sequence is a recursive sequence of numbers in which each number, after the first two, is the sum of the previous two. For example, 0, 1, 1, 2, 3, 5, 8, 13, 21, 34 and so on.

Leonardo Fibonacci (1170–c.1250) created the fibonacci sequence in 1225 to solve the puzzle of rabbit breeding rates. It has since been found to occur widely in nature – spirals of seeds on a sunflower head, the number of leaf buds on a stem, the number of petals in many flowers, and the spiral arrangements of pineapples. The sequence had been known in India since the 6th century and some of its ramifications weren't understood until long after Fibonacci's time.

Leonardo was probably the most talented Western mathematician of the Middle Ages. He was the son of a wealthy Italian merchant and customs official in Pisa. He travelled in North Africa with his father which is where he encountered Arabic mathematics.

He spread the word on his return to Europe and sparked a rejuvenation of the subject which had lain dormant during the Dark Ages. He wrote books on the topic despite the anti-Arab feelings in Europe thanks to the Crusades. He used the fraction notation of a horizontal bar for the first time in Europe in his first and most important book.

He has had an asteroid named in his honour.

Fosbury Flop

Dick Fosbury (born 1947) is the American high-jumper who invented the now standard backwards jump for high-jumping. He won the gold medal in the 1968 Mexico Olympics and his style of jump dominated the sport from then onwards.

Before Fosbury, jumpers used the straddle technique, western roll, and even the scissors jump to clear the bar. High jumpers of earlier years had to land in sandpits or low piles of mats so they needed to land on their feet in order to avoid injury. The introduction of deep foam matting in the early 1960s made the flop possible.

After he won, an American coach said "kids imitate champions. If they try to imitate Fosbury, he'll wipe out an entire generation of high-jumpers because they will all have broken necks."

The name of the jump came from a newspaper description in 1964 describing him as looking like a "fish flopping in a boat". Another even headlined him as "The World's Laziest High Jumper".

Galvanise

Galvanise is a process to cover iron or steel with a protective zinc coating to prevent rusting. It is also a verb meaning to stimulate into sudden action.

Galvanising was named for Luigi Galvani (1737-1798) who was an Italian physician, biologist, and philosopher who observed that the legs of frogs twitched when touched with metal objects. He thought this was due to animal electricity and he became a pioneer of the study of bioelectricity, the electrical signals from muscles and nerves.

Galvani didn't invent galvanizing. It is unclear who did. The earliest known example of galvanising iron is on 17th century Indian armour which is on display in the Royal Armouries Museum in the U.K..

As for stimulating action, well that's where the frogs come in again. Galvanising in this sense – the administration of electric shocks - was also known as faradism (after Michael Faraday) in the 19th century. Over time it gained a more metaphorical sense of firing a complacent person into motion. An electric shock would tend to have that effect.

Galvani's experiments inspired Volta to develop an early battery even though they disagreed respectfully on the causes of animal electricity. Towards the end of his life northern Italy was occupied by France and every university professor was required to swear an oath of loyalty to France. He refused, lost every position he held, and died in poverty.

Mary Shelley read about Galvani's experiments before writing Frankenstein but electrical re-animation is not mentioned in her classic novel, although it is referenced in the many movies inspired by her creation.

Galvani has a crater on the moon named after him.

Gladstone Bag

The Gladstone bag has flexible sides, generally of leather, on a rigid frame and two equal-sized compartments.

J.G. Beard is credited as the inventor the Gladstone bag in the mid 1800s at his shop in the City of Westminster. A staunch supporter of Gladstone, then Prime Minister, he named the bag after him, particularly as it was designed for travellers and Gladstone was renowned for his travels.

The bag is often called a doctor's bag and was linked to

several notorious murders in the late 1800s in London. Mary Poppins also carried a Gladstone, which seemed to have some tardis-like properties.

William Ewart Gladstone (1809-1898) was a four time British Prime Minister and Liberal. He was known as The Grand Old Man (GOM) and his political career lasted for 60 years. His last stint as Prime Minister ended when he was 84.

He was known for his rivalry with Disraeli who claimed his nickname abbreviation of GOM actually meant "God's only mistake". Queen Victoria wasn't a fan either, complaining that he "always addresses me as if I were a public meeting".

Despite a busy workload throughout his life, and eight children, he was a bibliophile who amassed a library of 32,000 books. His hobby was tree-felling for exercise. He was mocked for this destructive pursuit but always replanted saplings afterwards.

His coffin was transported on the London Underground (the Tube) on its way to his state funeral.

His life has been memorialised in town names and statues worldwide. One of the oddest tributes is his inclusion, as a non-player character, in "Assassin's Creed: Syndicate" where he and Disraeli can be seen engaged in a heated argument.

Guillotine

This bladed beheading device, originally called a louisette, was invented by Dr. Antoine Louis. It was used for the first time in 1792 to decapitate a highwayman called Pelletier.

Its eventual name came from another Frenchman – a humanitarian doctor called Joseph Ignace Guillotin (1738-1814) who argued passionately, during a debate in the French Assembly in 1789, for its introduction. He said it would be more humane than the current methods of capital punishment; hanging for commoners and beheading with a sword for nobility.

The guillotine wasn't unique to France. Similar devices were used in Scotland, England, Germany, and other European countries, usually for noble executions.

It also wasn't confined to the ten blood-soaked years of the Revolution when between 17,000 and 40,000 died beneath its slanted blade. The last execution by guillotine in France was in 1977.

After Guillotine's death his children tried to rename the device, without success, and were ultimately forced to change their own surname as they rejected the eponymous connection.

As a Frenchman carrying a ladder once said to me in Paris "Gardez la tête. Il y aurez une révolution!" Mind your head, there will be a revolution.

Heimlich Manoeuvre

Dr. Henry Judah Heimlich (1920-2016) used his own move, aged 96, in May 2016 to save the life of a fellow resident at his retirement home. The two had dinner together the following night to celebrate.

His technique for dislodging food or objects caught in people's throats has been credited with saving countless lives since he introduced it in 1974. Prior to that point, the standard remedy was to slap the person on the back but that could cause the obstruction to travel further down the gullet.

Heimlich was the uncle of Anson Williams who played Potsie in the 1970s TV hit "Happy Days".

Jacuzzi

A jacuzzi is a trademarked system of underwater jets

used to massage the body. The creator of the jacuzzi was Candido Jacuzzi (c. 1903-1986). He was born the youngest of seven brothers and six sisters. The family emigrated from Italy to California in the early 20th century. They seemed likely to prosper with a family aircraft engineering company, but when the Jacuzzi brother's monoplane crashed on its first flight their mother barred them from any more of that nonsense.

The brothers also worked in the field of fluid dynamics and developed a water pump for garden use. In 1943 one of the children was stricken with rheumatoid arthritis. They built a similar pump to work in their home bath-tub to ease the child's disease with hydrotherapy. They created a niche business selling the units to hospitals and schools.

In 1968 Roy Jacuzzi, a third generation member of the family, spotted the commercial potential of their invention outside of medical settings and the modern jacuzzi was born. By the 1970s he had added heating to the creation and hot tubs were on their way.

JCB

JCB is a trademark for a mechanical earth mover with a hydraulic shovel at the front and an excavator at the back.

Joseph Cyril Bamford (1916-2001) made his first vehicle in 1945, a tipping farm trailer to use with the new petrol tractors. He worked with a second-hand welding set and army surplus materials in a rented garage.

By the late 1950s he added hydraulics to his vehicles. His motto of "never content" drove the company onwards to where it's now a global brand employing 11,000 worldwide. Despite not recognising unions, the company was known for rewarding hard workers and had huge landscaped grounds around its main British plant for employees to use for shooting, fishing, swimming, and sailing.

The company is now headed by Sir Anthony Bamford, the eldest son of the original JCB, who was born on the day his father made his first vehicle.

Lear Jet

The quintessential private jet was designed by William Powell Lear's company. Lear (1902-1978) was a compulsive inventor who earned more than 120 patents during his life.

He struggled to gain an education, twice being expelled for showing up his teachers - once at high school and again when he returned to education after his U.S. navy service. As an adult he took four years of courses in just one year. As a result he was largely self-taught.

He rebuilt a Model T Ford as a summer project with his father, built his own radio, and taught himself Morse Code for fun. One of his early businesses used his insight to reduce the size of tuning coils in radios to one quarter of their normal size.

On a long road trip he helped Paul Galvin devise a new name for his Galvin Manufacturing company. They decided on Motorola.

When he needed a music source for his jets, he came up with 8-track music cartridges. He also created autopilots and automatic landing gear – technology that is now standard in aircraft.

Despite having a reputation for being "difficult", he had a sense of humour – naming his second daughter Shanda Lear (think chandelier).

Linux

This computer operating system, similar to unix but suitable for use on personal computers, was originally created by and named for Linus Torvalds (born 1969), a Finnish computer programmer.

Rather than copywriting it for financial gain, he made it available for public use on the internet in 1991. He asked other programmers to suggest improvements to him via email. Only 2% of the current version of linux was written by Torvalds who was a student at university when he wrote the original version.

Linux could have been named Freax, that was the working title for the project he'd chosen. He rejected Linux as too egotistical a title but one of the volunteers helping him renamed it without checking first and it stuck.

Tux, a cute little penguin, is the Linux mascot because Torvalds was once bitten by a penguin at a zoo in Australia.

Macadam

Tarmacadam is a compact layer of stones bound with tar. It is used typically as a road surface and is sometimes called tarmac for short.

Tarmacadam is named in honour of Scottish engineer John Loudon McAdam (1756-1836). It is said that when he was a small boy he used to lay out roads in his back garden. After spending some time in America he returned to the country estate he'd bought in Ayrshire but found the roads were a mess. He set to work to improve them and later did a similar job in Falmouth.

In 1815 he was appointed to construct roads around Bristol and in 1827 he was made surveyor general of all British metropolitan roads.

Tarmac was invented by Edgar Purnell Hooley (1860-1942) after seeing a spillage of tar on a pile of gravel.

Macadam's original road-building method involved the revolutionary notion of laying the road with a camber to enable water run-off. He also insisted on a size of stones relative to the common wheel widths of the day.

Mesmerise

To mesmerise someone is to fascinate, spellbind, or hypnotise them.

Austrian physicist and hypnotist Franz Anton Mesmer (1734-1815) studied and practised medicine in Vienna. He attributed his success to animal magnetism. He was intrigued by Newton's theory on gravity and believed the tidal influences of the planets could also operate on humans. He stroked his patients with magnets to allow his own magnetism to transfer across the ether to his patient and replenish their diminished levels.

He was exiled by the Viennese authorities and settled in Paris in 1778. Wearing purple robes, waving a wand, he attempted group cures and became hugely fashionable. In 1784 King Louis XVI appointed a scientific commission to investigate his practices. They concluded he was a charlatan and he had to flee once more. He spent the rest of his life in obscurity in Switzerland.

His supposed supernatural powers were almost certainly down to hypnotism.

Mesmer once helped a young Mozart perform his work in his garden when the original performance was cancelled. Mozart included a comic reference to Mesmer in "Così Fan Tutte" in return.

Montessori

Dr. Maria Montessori (1870-1952) was an Italian physicist and educator. She was the first woman to qualify with a degree in medicine, in 1896, from the University of Rome, although her father disagreed with her decision to pursue her education.

Maria came from a noble family. First working with mentally-disabled children and later opening schools for all children using her teaching principles of sensory materials and learning through play. She developed her theories as a result of observing how children learn naturally.

Her first class, for slum children in Florence, had 50-60 pupils aged 3-6. She gave the children fun puzzles, everyday tasks, and interesting activities within a room with child-sized furniture. She refined her methods for the rest of her life, working in Spain and India as well as her native Italy. She found her method worked with any age group and ability including special needs children and the extremely gifted.

When she was studying for her medical degree it was deemed inappropriate for her to do human anatomy dissections in the presence of her all-male classmates. She had to do hers alone, after hours. She took up tobacco smoking to mask the smell of formaldehyde.

Montessori had only one child, a son, with a fellow doctor. If she had married she would have had to stop working so they kept their relationship secret. Her son later helped her with her research.

She was nominated three times for the Nobel Peace Prize.

Morse Code

Morse code is a telegraphic system of communication where dots and dashes are combined to represent letters and numbers. The information is sent as a series of electrical signals. Short signals, represented by dots, are called dits while long signals, represented by dashes, are called dahs.

Morse code is named for its American inventor Samuel Finley Breese Morse (1791-1872). Morse graduated from Yale and travelled to London to become an artist. He achieved a good reputation as a portrait painter and exhibited at the Royal Academy in London. He founded the National Academy of Design in New York and was professor of painting and sculpting at New York University.

In 1827 his interests turned to electric telegraphy. He

dedicated twelve years to refining his concept. This devotion may have been as a result of poor communication resulting in him missing the death and burial of his first wife.

With backing from Congress he built the first telegraph line from Washington to Baltimore (1843-1844). The first message, on the 24th of May 1844, passed on the line was "What hath God wrought?"

Up to this time a message could only pass as quickly as a man on a horse could carry it. By 1851 there were over 50 telegraph companies in the U.S.. Morse patented Morse Code in 1854 after a legal battle. It was used as a standard for maritime communication until 1991.

On April Fool's Day 2012 Google announced the release of Gmail Tap saying it allowed users to send Morse Code from their mobile phones. Morse's great-great-grand-nephew Reed Morse, a Google engineer, was behind the prank and it later became a real product.

Nicotine

Nicotine, an addictive chemical compound found in tobacco, is named for French diplomat Jean Nicot (1530-1600). Nicot was ambassador to Portugal at the time when they were bringing back the early cargos of tobacco seeds to Europe from the New World. In 1560 he was given a tobacco plant from Florida which he grew and dispatched the seeds back to French nobles. When he returned to France he brought a ship full of tobacco with him and it became associated with his name. The tobacco plant, nicotiana tobacum, is also named for him.

Son of a notary, he managed to get a job working for the Keeper of the Great Seal of France, came to the notice of the King, became his private secretary, and eventually ambassador.

Ironically he became convinced of the healing properties of the tobacco plant, especially for cancerous tumours. He also sent some, in snuff form, to Catherine de Medici, the Queen of France, to treat her migraines.

Jean Nicot is also famous for having compiled one of the first ever French dictionaries, published in 1606. Ben Johnson's famous English dictionary was published in 1755.

Nobel Prize

The annual Nobel Prize was founded by Alfred Bernhard Nobel (1833-1896). He was a Swedish chemist, manufacturer, and philanthropist. He invented dynamite in 1866. He was a pacifist and thought it would form the core of a country's defence and bring peace to the world.

He made a fortune selling dynamite and trading in oil rights, thus enabling his will to fund the annual award in the fields of physics, chemistry, medicine, literature and peace since 1901. In 1969 an additional award in economics was introduced (and fictionally awarded to President Jed Bartlett in "The West Wing").

Alfred spoke five languages fluently by the age of 17 and held 355 patents by the time of his death. Known for his scientific work, he was a keen poet and playwright also.

His father created the first sea mines for the Czar of Russia which were deployed in the Crimean War. While the family lived in Russia, Alfred's father created central heating and their home was the first house in the country to have it installed. Alfred was tutored at home with his siblings and never studied at university. He learned by working with the leading scientists of the day.

Alfred's dynamite soon turned to warfare usage as well as mining. However his writings on the subject of war show that he believed if both sides had devastating weapons then no war would take place – the mutually assured destruction idea. He didn't live to see how incorrect that notion was proven in World War One.

Nobel also has an element named in his honour.

Nobellium, an artificially created element, was named for him in 1957. The discovering scientists did *not* win the Nobel prize for their work.

Orrery

An orrery is a mechanical device which shows the relative positions and orbits of the planets and moons around the sun in our solar system.

It was invented by mathematician George Graham (1671-1751) in 1704. He sent the device to instrument maker John Rowley (d. 1728) who built a copy and presented it to his patron Charles Boyle, the 4th Earl of Orrery (1676-1731) and named the device in his honour.

The original orrery only showed the earth, moon and sun but Boyle's patronage ensured the fame of the device and the other planets were soon added.

George Graham's other works included improvements to pendulum clocks, instruments for famous astronomers, and the great mural quadrant at Greenwich Observatory, London for Edmond Halley of Halley's Comet fame.

A giant orrery is used in the climactic scenes of the Lara Croft Tomb Raider movie in 2001. Armagh Observatory in Northern Ireland has a precise human orrery where people stand in for the moving planets.

Pamphlet

A pamphlet is an unbound printed publication with a paper cover. Its name comes from a 12th century love poem called "Pamphilus Seu de Amore" which translates as "Pamphilus, or on Love". Pamphilus was a man's first name. This short Latin poem was very popular and the poem became known just as Pamphilet, the pamflet, and finally pamphlet.

The idea of a pamphlet being a short treatise on a matter of current interest came about in the 16th century particularly during the Reformation period, although religious pamphlets are more likely to be called tracts. Martin Luther, for example, was a prolific and effective pamphleteer. However Elizabethan England they were also used for romantic fiction, scurrilous personal abuse, social and literary criticism.

In the 18th century, pamphlets were influential in pre-revolutionary America on political topics and they played a role in the French Revolution also.

As the availability of newspapers rose, pamphlets changed course again and are commonly used now as the voice of specific government departments, for health campaigns etc..

Pamphlet writers of the past include Luther, George Bernard Shaw, Thomas Paine, Voltaire, Rousseau, and Jonathan Swift.

Pascal

Blaise Pascal (1623-1662) was a French mathematician, inventor, physicist, and philosopher who formulated Pascal's triangle in probability theory, made discoveries in fluid mechanics, invented a hydraulic press and a calculating machine.

Pascal was a child prodigy who was educated by his father, a high-level tax collector. Starting in his teens, and after 50 prototypes, he created twenty machines called Pascal's calculators or Pascalines. He made them to help his father calculate the taxes.

These mechanical calculators were created almost two hundred years before Charles Babbage's famous difference engine – the father of modern computers. Pascal's work built on earlier efforts by Wilhelm Schickard in 1623. Due to the expense of making them and the difficulty of using them the Pascalines became a play thing for the rich of France and didn't gain widespread use.

Both a computer programming language and the metric unit of pressure are named in his honour. His theorem, devised aged 16, is still known by his name in mathematics today, much to the irritation of his contemporary rival Descartes.

He created a primitive roulette wheel in his search for a perpetual motion machine.

He also created an early form of syringe and created the first bus route – a carriage with many seats operating in Paris in 1661.

In 1654 he corresponded with Pierre de Fermat on the topic of gambling theory and between them they pretty much invented probability theory. Later that year, after a religious experience, he renounced mathematics in favour of philosophy.

Plimsolls and the Plimsoll Line

The plimsoll line is the mark painted on a ship's hull to indicate the safe loading level of the ship at a glance. If the mark is underwater, the ship is overloaded. It is named in honour of Samuel Plimsoll (1824-1898) who was a shipping reformer.

Plimsoll left school at an early age, began work as a clerk in a brewery, and worked his way up to become the manager. He was then a coal dealer but went bankrupt and lived in very reduced circumstances which sparked his sympathy for the poor when his fortunes recovered.

In 1868 he was elected MP for the land-locked constituency of Derby. He called the routinely overloaded ships of his day "coffin ships". They were often heavily insured and the unscrupulous owners risked the lives of their crew knowing they wouldn't lose money if they sank. He campaigned for safety improvements in maritime traffic despite the large number of ship-owner members of parliament.

In 1872 a compromise bill was going to be introduced to deal with the issue and Plimsoll accepted it, reluctantly. When Disraeli announced the bill was to be dropped Plimsoll called his parliamentary colleagues villains and shook his fist in the Speaker's face, outraged that pressure from ship-owners had stifled the new law.

Eventually he apologised for his unbecoming behaviour but popular opinion admired his honesty and a year later the government was forced to make rigorous inspections of ships compulsory. The Plimsoll Line was adopted in the same year. It is likely that this simple line of paint has saved thousands of lives at sea.

In the 1920s plimsolls, rubber-soled canvas shoes, came to bear his name because the line of the rubber sole reminded wearers of the plimsoll line.

Pulitzer Prize

The Pulitzer Prize is actually a set of prizes awarded for achievements in journalism, literature, and music.

The Pulitzer Prize was initiated by Hungarian born, U.S. newspaper publisher Joseph Pulitzer (1847-1911) who was one of the first to call for university-trained journalists. Pulitzer emigrated to America in 1864 and spent a year in the Union army before settling in St. Louis and founding "The Post-Dispatch" newspaper in 1878. In 1883 he moved to New York and established a new paper called "World".

The prizes were established thanks to his will, where he funded a school of journalism in Columbia University. The prizes have been running since 1917 and consist of a series of scholarships and awards for things like best editorial of the year, best reporting of the year with the test being accuracy and terseness, an American biography, book on the history of the United States etc.. He provided for a board to amend the rules if required by changing times and to refuse to award a prize if the high standard wasn't met in a given year. The board has amended the prizes over time and they now include poetry, photography, and music.

Although large circulation broadsheets often capture the awards, many smaller newspapers have also been honoured and some online media.

Pulitzer regarded himself as a self-made man. His struggles as a young journalist made him determined to support the next generation in accessing professional training and rewards.

Pulitzer's path into the Union army was a strange one. His frail health and poor eyesight saw the 6'2" seventeen year old rejected by the Austrian army, the French Foreign Legion, and the British Army. When he met a recruiting agent in Germany for the Union Army he jumped at the chance. In order to deny the agent of their bounty for recruiting him, he jumped ship early and swam to shore to sign up so he could keep his own enlistment bonus.

His break into journalism came after his stint in the cavalry. He was studying English and law in St. Louis' mercantile library when he observed a game of chess between two regular visitors. He critiqued a move and the players engaged him in conversation. They were the editors of the leading German language newspaper in the city and they offered him a job. Four years later, having proven his journalistic ability, he gained a controlling share in the failing paper and began his climb to the top of the business.

His papers crusaded against corruption and named themselves champions of the people. "The World" raised the money, via public subscriptions, to build the pedestal for the Statue of Liberty in New York.

He sacrificed his own health with his long work hours and circulation battles with William Randolph Hearst's "Journal". No target was too high for his corruption exposés, including a fraudulent payment from President Theodore Roosevelt's government to the French Panama Canal Company in 1909. Retreating from the public eye, he continued to run his business with a keen eye until his death aboard his yacht in 1911.

Pullman Car or Seat

George Mortimer Pullman (1831-1897) was an American engineer and millionaire industrialist whose name is inextricably linked with luxury train travel.

He was born in New York and dropped out of school at 14. He worked first as a clerk and then with his father moving houses to new foundations during the widening of the Erie Canal. He moved to Chicago as a young engineer, formed a partnership, and worked to raise the buildings of central Chicago to a higher level above the new sewerage system, including moving a six-story brick hotel while the guests were still inside.

After sleeping in his train seat on a trip from Buffalo to Westfield, New York, he was inspired to design his signature creation, a railway sleeping car – the Pullman sleeper - completing it in 1864. The railcar had sleeping berths for every passenger which folded away during the day. There were washrooms for men and women at the end of the car.

After President Lincoln's assassination Pullman arranged to have his body carried in one of his train carriages from Washington D.C. to Springfield, which granted him huge exposure as hundreds of thousands of Americans lined the route as a mark of respect.

Orders flooded in despite his cars costing five times the amount a normal railroad car would cost.

To match the comfort of the Pullman cars, his passengers needed someone to run various services for them during their journeys; collecting tickets, converting the berth for sleeping, sending wires, and fetching sandwiches. Pullman recruited a team of well-respected African Americans for the role and he became the single largest employer of that ethnicity after the American Civil War.

He operated more than 700 Pullman cars on railways around the country.

In 1880 he bought land south of Chicago for a new factory. He built a company town (much like the Quaker chocolate-making family that built Bourneville in the U.K.) with accommodation for his workers. It also featured shops, churches, theatres, parks, a hotel, and a library.

Originally intended as a way to promote worker welfare, Pullman ruled the town as his personal fiefdom. He controlled the newspapers and prohibited public speeches and open discussion. His inspectors entered homes to check for cleanliness and evicted those that failed with only ten days' notice.

In 1894 when demand for the railcars reduced Pullman cut wages and jobs but didn't reduce rents in his model town. Inevitably the workers went on strike. Pullman refused to negotiate.

Worker unrest and issues over railway mail deliveries increased. Violence erupted. Federal troops went in to protect the mail and 34 people died. The strike leader landed in jail and Pullman was severely criticised by the presidential investigation. He was forced to hand ownership of his town to the city of Chicago.

Pullman died of a heart attack three years after the strike. His family arranged an unusual burial for him which took two days to complete. He was buried in a lead-lined mahogany coffin which was then sealed in a large block of concrete. They feared he might be dug up by disgruntled former employees.

Pullman seats in cinemas do not appear to be linked to Pullman himself, except as a sign of comfort and luxury.

Robot

{with thanks to Rick Ellrod at https://rickellrod.com/}

The word robot comes from the 1921 Czech play "R.U.R." by Karel Čapek (1890-1938) whose title translates as "Rossum's Universal Robots". This sci-fi play introduced the word robot to the English language. By 1923 it had been translated into 23 languages so it's safe to say it was a hit.

It tells the story of robotii made in a factory from synthetic organic materials. They are cyborg/clone creatures who can be mistaken for humans and can think for themselves. At first they are happy to be slaves for the humans but they rebel and it leads to the extinction of humanity.

Karel said afterwards that his brother Josef was the true inventor of the word. In Czech robota means forced labour of the kind serfs had to do on their master's land and it is derived from the word rab which means slave.

In 2015 a team of mainly high-school students created an all-robot cast production of the play using Lego mindstorm robots with the students providing the voices.

Karel was nominated for the Nobel Prize for literature seven times but he never won it. He worked primarily as a journalist and when forced by ill-health to be a non-combatant in World War I he became an outspoken anti-fascist.

In 1938 it became clear that his homeland would be invaded and he was declared public enemy number two by the Gestapo but refused to go into exile in England. While doing repairs on his home, he contracted a common cold which developed into pneumonia and died. Several months later, after the invasion, the Gestapo turned up to arrest him and took his brother instead when they were informed of Karel's death. His brother Josef died in Bergen-Belsen concentration camp in April 1945.

Saxophone

A sax is a keyed woodwind instrument with a brass body. It was invented by Belgian inventor and musician Adolphe Sax (1814-1894) who was working in his father's instrument workshop in the 1840s. It was first shown to the public in 1844 and music was written for it by Berlioz and Bizet but it is mostly used for jazz and dance music now.

Sax, who played the clarinet and flute himself, also created the saxtromba, saxtuba, and the saxhorn, but none of them gained an audience. The saxhorn is still sometimes played and laid the groundwork for the flugelhorn which is played in brass bands.

Sax created his own instruments from a young age as both his parents were instrument designers themselves. His neighbours called him "little sax, the ghost" when he was growing up as he survived so many near-death experiences.

He fell from a height of three floors onto stone, burnt himself in a gunpowder explosion, survived poisoning and suffocation thanks to varnished items in his bedroom, was hit on the head by a cobblestone, and fell into a river and barely survived.

His patents were challenged and the legal costs drove

him to bankruptcy twice. He died in poverty in Paris.

Silhouette

A silhouette is a portrait method which shows a dark shape outlined against a white background.

French politician Étienne de Silhouette (1709-1767) had to cut government spending in 1759 thanks to the expenses of the Seven Years War against Britain. His name became synonymous with doing something on the cheap "à la silhouette". His tax policies were austere in the extreme and unlikely to make him a champion of the people.

Meantime shade or profile portraits, as they were then known, became popular at court. Artists using this ancient technique (used in ancient Greek and Egyptian art) produced quick and cheap portraits. They attended the aristocrats' balls and captured the latest fashions and hair-styles.

It is possible Silhouette himself practised the art-form but either way, the portraits became linked to his name. The heavily-taxed peasant class began wearing only black to mock his paper cut-outs and they protested they were dressing à la silhouette – "we are shadows, too poor to wear colour".

The art survived the French Revolution better than the nobility did and it persists to this day with certain silhouette artists being very collectable, although photography's cheap portraits largely replaced it in the early 1900s. Silhouette himself didn't last in the Controller-General role and died before the French Revolution which reversed many of his taxes.

Teddy Bear

One of the most famous eponyms is that teddy bears are named for President Theodore Roosevelt (1858-1919) but the full story is not widely known outside America.

Roosevelt was a famous hunter. Many of his stuffed trophies are displayed in the Natural History Museum in New York. Governor Andrew H Longino invited him in 1902 to go hunting in Mississippi. Three days into the trip all the hunters had spotted bear, except for the guest of honour.

The next day the guides tracked down an old black bear. Their dogs trailed the bear for some distance and brought it down. The guides tied the bear to a willow tree and called for the President.

Roosevelt took one look at the bear and refused to shoot it as it would be unsportsmanlike. However since it was injured and suffering he asked that it be put down.

The story hit the newspapers and became a cartoon in the "Washington Post" by Clifford K. Berryman. In fact Berryman included a bear motif in many of his future cartoons of Roosevelt and they forged the link to the president in the popular imagination.

Around the same time a candy story owner in Brooklyn, New York called Morris Michtom saw the cartoons and had an idea. He took two toy bears his wife had made and put them in his shop window. He asked permission of the president to label them as "Teddy's Bears" and they were a huge hit. They began to manufacture them and the company eventually became the Ideal Novelty and Toy Company which later produced the eponymous Rubik's cube.

Meanwhile in Germany, Margaret Steiff was making her living by sewing stuffed toy animals. An American saw her toy bears and ordered thousands. These bears also came to be called Teddy Bears and the name stuck. Steiff bears are highly collectible but none of that original order have been found, fueling rumours that they were ship-wrecked.

Theodore Roosevelt was born a sickly child with severe asthma but he embraced a strenuous outdoorsy lifestyle.

He lived an extraordinary life including promoting women's rights in his Harvard undergraduate work (he felt full equality was the only way and they shouldn't have to take their husband's name), running a cattle ranch in Dakota, serving with the Rough Riders in the Spanish-American War, becoming the youngest ever U.S. President when President McKinley was assassinated, starting construction of the Panama Canal, creating many national parks, and nearly dying of a tropical disease in the Amazon basin.

He won a Nobel Prize in 1906 for his successful efforts to end the Russo-Japanese War. The prize, the first ever won by an American, is on display in the Roosevelt Room (named for him and FDR), exactly as referenced in the popular TV series "The West Wing".

In 1911 Roosevelt was presented with an honourary degree at Cambridge University, England and he later described how much the students there reminded him of his fellow students. When he arrived he walked through the students on a pathway and at the end of the path they had placed a large friendly teddy bear with his hand outstretched in welcome. Later when he was being conferred with the degree they rigged a pulley system to lower a teddy bear onto his head.

Apparently they had lowered a monkey (hopefully a soft toy too) onto Charles Darwin's head under the same circumstances.

Tony Award

The Tony Award is the American theatre award named for Antoinette Perry, known as Tony (1888-1946). She made her theatre debut in 1905 and was a successful actress, producer, and chair of the American Theatre Council.

The award which began in 1947 was named for Antoinette because she had recently passed away and had been a stalwart of the theatre scene during the war years. Initially the award was a scroll plus a money clip for male recipients and scroll plus a mirror compact for the female recipients. When they designed a medal it had the theatre masks on one side and Tony's profile on the reverse side.

Many famous actors and actresses have won Tony awards and the elite few have managed the full sweep to be EGOTs – Emmy, Grammy, Oscar, and Tony winners. That list includes Audrey Hepburn, Mel Brooks, Whoopi Goldberg, and John Gielgud.

The youngest Tony winner was Frankie Michaels for "Mame". Dolores Gray won for her performance in "Carnival in Flanders" in 1953, a musical that closed after only six nights.

Tony Perry joined her uncle's touring theatre company at

the age of 15 and rose swiftly from selling tickets to leading lady. She married a former boyfriend from home at the peak of her career and began investing in productions. Her profits combined with her inheritance from her husband enabled her to bail out actors in money difficulties and delve into a directing career with her long term friend Brock Pemberton.

They landed their first break with "Strictly Dishonourable", selling movie rights and selling out the theatre. A month later the stock market crashed and she found herself two million dollars in debt.

Never an easy woman to keep down, she worked her way back over seven years. Then she funded shows for overseas troops during World War Two, supported new playwrights, and worked to establish a national actor's school.

Apparently her luck with horse gambling helped with the finances many times.

Venn Diagram

A Venn diagram shows the logical connections between a collection of different sets as a series of overlapping circles. They are used to teach basic set theory and to illustrate set relationships in probability, logic, statistics, and computer science.

Venn diagrams were conceived by John Venn around 1880. He never called them Venn diagrams, referring to them as Eulerian Circles - a name which indicated the roots of his idea in Euler diagrams in the 1700s. In fact such diagrams were in use since the 1200s but Venn developed them significantly and brought them to a form we would recognise today.

John Venn (1834-1923) was descended from a long line of church evangelicals and he was brought up in a very strict home. His mother died when he was three. He studied mathematics at Cambridge where he became a fellow and president of his college. He also became an Anglican priest, following in the family business, although he later resigned from the clergy having decided it didn't match his philosophical beliefs.

There is a stained glass Venn diagram window in the dining hall of his college at Cambridge to commemorate his work.

Wendy House

A Wendy house is a small model house for kids to play in. It can either be a plastic construction or something more solid and is typically a one room home with no furniture inside. It is named for the character Wendy Darling in the play "Peter Pan, or The Boy Who Wouldn't Grow Up" by the Scottish novelist and dramatist Sir James Matthew Barrie (1860-1937). He also published the play in novel format later.

In the play Wendy is shot by Tootles, one of the Lost Boys, when she arrives in Neverland so Peter Pan and the boys build the house around her for shelter. The house itself was inspired by the wash-house behind Barrie's childhood home and he created the prop house for the first production of the play.

Toy manufacturers created replicas of the house and they have been a classic toy in gardens ever since.

Barrie is often credited with inventing the girl's name Wendy as it wasn't really used before he wrote his play. It is believed that he took the name from a phrase used by the daughter of a friend of his, Margaret Henley. She called Barrie her "friendy-wendy". She died when she was five.

Barrie wrote a short play called "When Wendy Grew Up – An Afterthought" which shows Wendy as a mother allowing her daughter Jane to go with Peter, trusting her to make the same decision - to return and grow up - as she once did.

Peter Pan was inspired by Barrie's relationship with the Llewelyn-Davies family of five boys to whom Barrie became guardian after their parents' deaths. He also drew on his mother's notion that his older brother David, who died when Barrie was six, would remain ever young.

In 1929 Barrie gave all the rights to "Peter Pan" to Great Ormond Street Children's Hospital so they receive the royalties each time the play is produced and from the sale of Peter Pan books and other products.

Although he and his wife were childless they had loved and supported the hospital for many years. He even once claimed that Peter Pan had been a patient at the hospital and it was *his* idea to donate the royalties.

The term Wendy House is also used in South Africa for basic homes, often built in the back gardens of other houses and typically occupied by low earners.

Zeppelin

A zeppelin is an airship and is named for the German general and aeronautical pioneer Count Ferdinand von Zeppelin (1838-1917).

The Count served in the American Civil War and the Franco-Prussian War. He witnessed Union army balloons in 1863 when he visited the U.S. as a military observer during the Civil War. He retired from the army in 1891 and developed his interest in airships and by 1900 had built the first rigid airship. He funded his later experiments thanks to public donations as huge national pride swelled for this new invention.

Between 1910 and 1914 zeppelins were widely used to carry passengers in Germany, as shown in "Indiana Jones and The Last Crusade".

During World War I the Germans used them to bomb Britain despite their vulnerability to anti-aircraft fire. They were also used to spot mines at sea. Downed zeppelins gave the British valuable information for developing their own airships.

After the war there were restrictions placed on German construction of zeppelins but over time they were eased and by the 1930s services flew from Germany to North America and Brazil. Originally, the art-deco spire of the

Empire State building was to be a tethering point for such airships but high winds made it impractical.

Early ships had no heating for passengers and they flew in freezing misery but later versions moved the passenger accommodation inside the main ship and devised a heating system. They even, incredibly, had a smoking room, which was air-locked for safety.

In August 1929 the Graf Zeppelin circumnavigated the globe in 21 days. It also completed a seven day research trip to the Arctic in 1931.

In 1936 the Graf Zeppelin was surpassed by the Hindenburg, the largest airship ever built. It was designed to use non-flammable helium but supplies of the gas were controlled by the U.S. and they refused to export it. The fateful decision to fill her with highly flammable hydrogen was taken. Less than a year later, with several Nazi propaganda missions under her belt, the Hindenburg landed in America and her tail fin caught fire. Within seconds the whole ship was aflame and 35 of the 97 people on board died. The investigation said the gas ignited thanks to a static electricity spark but sabotage was also mooted.

Airships have been revived in more recent times with helium (a non-flammable gas) and are now called Zeppelin NT (new technology) airships. One company operated a passenger service with them from 2008-2012 and they are popular for sightseeing trips in Austria.

British rock group Led Zeppelin took the name in defiance of critics when they were told they would go down like a lead balloon.

Conclusion

Getting your name into the dictionary isn't an easy task and neither is inventing something of significant use to the world, but if you invent it you usually get to name it and some of these inventors also ended up pretty rich too. Becoming an inventor could be a good move.

6
Location, Location, Location

If you've ever bought or sold a house you'll know that location matters. It's the same with eponyms. You may not be able to get your own name into the dictionary, but have you considered your home-town? Throughout history certain places have become famous enough to lend their name to the English language. Perhaps your town could be the next one.

Such a language addition actually has its own term – toponym – which comes from the Greek words topos (place) and nym (name). You might have heard of topography, that's a related word. Those of us interested in place-names are toponymists studying toponymy.

If you're interested in the names of seas and oceans then you're looking at hydronyms and oronyms for mountains and hills.

For the moment, however, let's have a look at the places around the world who have contributed to the English dictionary.

Bermuda Shorts

The story of these formal dress shorts begins with a very British cup of tea and two world wars.

In World War I the British navy established their North Atlantic headquarters on the island of Bermuda. Local man Nathanial Coxon owned a tea-shop in Bermuda and it quickly saw a boom in custom from naval officers. The steam from all the tea pots made it a hot spot in a bad way and his staff complained their uniform of a smart navy blazer teamed with khaki trousers was stifling. Coxon, a thrifty man, shortened all the trousers to just above the knee.

When Rear Admiral Mason Berridge took his tea at Coxon's he admired the look, dubbed them Bermuda Shorts, and adopted them for his officers. He always gave credit to Coxon, who was later awarded an OBE (Order of the British Empire). The Royal Navy uniform still includes the shorts.

The idea of wearing knee-high socks with the shorts came about in World War II. Two bank managers in Bermuda ordered the shorts for their employees, partly due to clothing and fabric shortages in the war, and paired them with long socks. The look was a fashion smash, local shops copied it and it is now the island's national dress. Businessmen wear the short and sock combo all year round. During the Olympic opening ceremony the Bermudian team usually sport red Bermuda shorts as red is the main colour in their flag.

Not everyone was happy about so much leg being on show so policemen were armed with a tape measure and a ticket book and sent out to ensure that the menfolk weren't showing more than six inches of leg.

Bikini

On the 5th of July 1946 French designer Louis Réard (1897-1984) unveiled a daring two-piece swimsuit in Paris and he named it the bikini after the Bikini Atoll in the Pacific Ocean which had hosted an U.S. atomic test earlier that week.

Réard was a gifted marketeer as well as designer, happy to hop on the coat-tails of the headline-grabbing tests. He also claimed you couldn't call a two-piece a real bikini unless it could pass through a wedding ring.

In his hunt for a model willing to bare nearly all in front of the world's press, he chose Micheline Bernardini - a Parisian showgirl/exotic dancer. He used newspaper style print on the fabric as a reference to the headlines he knew the garment would produce and unsurprisingly the bikini was a huge hit. Bernardini received 50,000 fan letters.

The two-piece wasn't new. Greek and Roman women were depicted wearing them in art from antiquity. Modern Europeans had worn them as halter tops with shorts during the 1930s but beach life was essentially impossible in Europe during World War II thanks to coastline fortifications and land mines in the sand. The 1946 bikini marked a post-war return to the shoreline.

Young women wearing the new fashion created a scandal along the beaches of Europe. Spain and Italy passed prohibitions against them but by the 1950s, perhaps thanks to iconic photographs of Brigit Bardot at the 1953 Cannes Film Festival, the bikini had eroded resistance.

The bikini won over America in the early 1960s with the rise of a younger, liberated generation who bopped along to the Beach Boys and Brian Hyland's "Itsy, Bitsy, Teenie, Weenie, Yellow Polka Dot Bikini".

Bristol Fashion

The phrase "ship-shape and Bristol Fashion", from the 1800s, has surprising links to the British slave trade.

Bristol was a great port on the so-called "triangular trade". Merchants exported manufactured goods to Africa where the ships then collected slaves to sell in the Caribbean plantations, where they picked up cargos of raw materials like sugar, cotton, chocolate, and tobacco bound for Europe. On each leg of the triangular journey the ship-owners made a profit. Slavery wasn't abolished in the British Empire until 1833.

The slave ships not only stank but also carried disease, so the citizens of the prosperous merchant town of Bristol wouldn't allow them to dock until they were cleaned and made tidy. Before they entered the harbour the ships were inspected to ensure they were ship-shape and Bristol fashion.

Additionally, Bristol port had the second highest tidal range in the world at the time – 13 metres (43 feet) – so ships moored in the area would be aground at low tide and tilt to one side. If everything wasn't tied down and stowed away properly it would be chaotic.

Charleston

The Charleston, a popular 1920s jazz dance with toe-in-heel-out twisting steps, was mentioned as early as 1903 and was originally an African American folk dance known throughout the American South. It is especially associated with the town of Charleston in South Carolina.

Around 1920 it was adopted by professional dancers and it made a big impression when featured in the 1923 musical "Running Wild" with a tune by composer/pianist James P. Johnson. It became a national, and international, craze. Johnson said he was inspired by a beat he heard from Charleston dockworkers.

In the acclaimed movie of "The Great Gatsby" released in 2013 and based on the famous novel by F. Scott Fitzgerald party guests are seen dancing the Charleston in the background when Gatsby introduces himself to Nick Caraway, but the novel is set in 1922 *before* the craze took off.

Corbett

Originally a Corbett was any Scottish hill between 2,500 and 2,999 feet (762-914m) in height with a 500 foot separation from peaks around it. Nowadays this name can be applied to any such hill in the British Isles.

The name comes from John Rooke Corbett (1876-1949). In this case the man gave the name to the hill and the dictionary, rather than the hill giving the word to the dictionary.

Corbett compiled a list of the Scottish Corbetts and climbed all 219 of them. The list was only published after his death when his sister passed it on to the Scottish Mountaineering Club.

He was also the fourth person to "bag" all the Munros in 1930 and the first Englishman to do so.

His father established one of Britain's first daycare nurseries for working mothers.

Coventry

{with thanks to Nell Jenda}

The British phrase "sending someone to Coventry" meant you would ignore them, refusing to acknowledge their presence or their utterances. It was a common peer punishment in classic Enid Blyton or Angela Brazil boarding school stories which is where I found it but it dates back to the 1600s.

The story from "The History of the Rebellion and Civil Wars in England" by Edward Hyde, 1st Earl of Clarendon, says that the phrase originated in the 17th century when

Cromwell sent some royalist prisoners, captured in Birmingham, to the then small town of Coventry. The locals, all parliamentarian supporters of Cromwell, shunned them.

Sending to Coventry was also used as a punishment for minor misbehaviour in the army. When the errant soldier did their penance and apologised or bought a round of drinks they would be welcomed back from their fictional journey to Coventry.

The phrase was common during industrial disputes in the mid 1900s in Britain. Anyone deemed to be unsupportive of the workforce would find themselves ostracised by their workmates. Many of these disputes occurred in the car industry and especially at British Leyland which was largely based in Coventry. This led to the bizarre circumstance of people who were born and bred in Coventry being sent there figuratively by their colleagues.

Coventry also contributed another, non-eponymous, phrase to the dictionary – the "peeping tom". This fictional character from the tale of Lady Godiva, was a Coventry resident and his story is explained in more detail in the Popular Phrase chapter.

Davy Jones' Locker

Davy Jones' locker is at the bottom of the sea and is mariners' slang for the final resting place of drowned sailors.

It is unlikely that there was a real Davy Jones, despite the character in "The Pirates of the Caribbean" movies. Various candidates exist, however.

Jones may be a corruption of the biblical figure, Jonah, who was swallowed by a whale. Jonah was seen as a bad luck figure by superstitious seafarers, probably because his tale involved a boat in peril as a result of his presence aboard it.

The patron saint of sailors is St. David (also the patron saint of Wales, he's a busy chap) and David is often shortened to Davy, so that might give us the first name. Jones is also a popular Welsh surname. Dying is a way of joining the saints so the locker could be heaven in this case.

"Brewer's Dictionary of Phrase and Fable" from 1898 claims the term comes from a combination of things – the locker being the safe place for a sailor to store something (their soul), Jones from the story of Jonah (who was sent overboard) and Davy from duffy (a word for a ghost or evil spirit in the West Indies).

An alternative tale springs from a 1594 ballad that would connect time-wise with Davy Jones' origin. The song "Jones' Ale is Newe" tells of a certain Davy Jones who owned a pub of the time. He gathered up drunk sailors in his bar and stored them safely in the ale lockers at the back of the inn, then sold them to the press gang. Sailors were always in short supply and a fee would be paid for men. The drunks woke aboard ship and had to serve out their voyage while Jones pocketed their sign-on fees.

In JM Barrie's novel "Peter and Wendy", Captain Hook sings a song; "Yo ho, yo ho, the frisky plank. You walks along it so. Till it goes down and you goes down to Davy Jones below!"

There is a long-standing tradition of celebrating crossing the equator by paying homage to Davy Jones. Those who have crossed it before play the part of Neptune and Neptune's sons or shellbacks. This is observed in many national navies. Those who are new to the crossing are called pollywogs. The ceremony can get rough and has been prohibited in a few cases.

Dumdum

Dumdum has two meanings. The first is idiot as demonstrated by the Easter Island statue in "Night at the

Museum" who constantly asks the night guard for a "gum gum, Dumdum". The second is an expanding bullet.

The bullets are named for the towns of North and South Dumdum, six kilometres north of Calcutta, India. Their names, which sound odd in English, make perfect sense in Hindi. A damdama is a raised mound or battery in Hindi and the towns housed the Bengal Artillery headquarters. Dumdum bullets were developed and tested there in the 1890s.

The British Army planned to use the devastating fragmenting bullets in the Boer War (1899-1902) but were stopped by the Second Hague Conference of 1899. However by World War II the bullets had crept into use even though it was technically a war crime. Allied troops captured at Dunkirk were carrying them and German propaganda of the time highlighted their use by French troops.

Everest

Everest is used as an adjective to describe the pinnacle of achievement in many fields which is unsurprising as it's the highest peak in the world.

Mount Everest stands at 8,848m (29,028 feet) in Nepal on the border with Tibet and is named for Sir George Everest (1790-1866). The border runs right across the summit.

Sir George, as Surveyor General of India, was the first to undertake detailed mapping of the area including the Himalayas. He didn't want the mountain named after him because it couldn't be written in Hindi or pronounced by locals.

Everest has two other names – Sagarmāthā in Nepal and Chomolungma in Tibet.

Local man Tenzing Norgay and Edmund Hillary from New Zealand made the first successful ascent of the mountain on the 29th of May 1953. They have been followed by more than 4,000 others since then, some of them climbing Everest multiple times. They paused at the top to bury some sweets in the snow and to take a photograph. When Hillary returned to Kathmandu he discovered he'd been given an OBE by the Queen of England.

Climbers seeking the summit of Everest typically spend a sizable amount of time in the Death Zone – altitudes higher than 8,000 metres (26,000 feet) where oxygen levels are a third of normal, high winds are a danger, and frostbite is a risk too. It usually takes climbers 12 hours to walk the last two kilometres and acclimatisation to the altitude will take weeks. Without it a sea-level dweller would pass out in minutes. There are over 200 corpses on Everest but removal of items from its slopes can be perilous. In one case the efforts to remove a corpse resulted in two more deaths.

The youngest climber to summit Everest was Malavath Purna from India when she was 13 years old.

The Sherpa people believe Mount Everest is blessed with spiritual energy and one should show respect to this sacred landscape and avoid impure thoughts when climbing there.

Frankfurter

Frankfurter entered the dictionary as a term for a hot dog directly from German. A frankfurter wurst was a smoked beef and pork sausage from Frankfurt am Main. The name of the city translates as the ford of the Franks on the River Main.

Sausages have a long and glorious history. They were even mentioned in Homer's "Odyssey" (9th century B.C.). They were made all over Europe and although Vienna has a pretty good claim to the original hot-dog (wieners and all that) Frankfurt is holding its ground. They even celebrated 500 years of the frankfurter in 1987 and claim the first one was created five years before Columbus sailed to the New World.

It is likely that German immigrants brought their sausages to America in the 1860s. They rapidly became a popular street food. By the 1870s there are records of cart vendors selling them with milk rolls and sauerkraut on the streets of New York.

In 1893 the so-called dachshund sausages were a hit at the Chicago Colombian Exposition because they could be eaten on the go. They became standard fair at baseball games for the same reason. From dachshund to dog was a short hop leaving hungry fans with hotdogs.

A long-time feature of New York's Coney Island is Nathan's Hot Dog stand (established in 1916). Each year, since the 1970s, on the 4th of July they host a hotdog eating contest. The rules are simple, whoever eats the most hotdogs in ten minutes is the winner. Joey Chestnut ate 70 in 1916.

Gibraltar

Gibraltar's name comes from gebel Tarik, meaning Tarik's mountain. Tarik was a Moorish chief who conquered the place in 711 and built a castle on the rock.

The Moors held it until 1309 when the Spanish took it for a while, then the Moors again and the Spanish held it from 1462 until 1704 when it was seized by Sir George Rooke for Britain. By 1783 Spain decided to forego her claim to the rock in favour of her claims on Florida and Minorca (Spain sold Florida to the U.S.A. in 1809).

In total there were 13 sieges of Gibraltar throughout the rock's erratic history of ownership, including one during the Second World War. As a result you may raise a glass to the Siege of Gibraltar on any date in the calendar year – the perfect excuse for a drink.

Gordian Knot

A Gordian knot is a complex and perhaps insurmountable problem. It's a phrase that dates back to the time of Alexander the Great (356-323 B.C.). In 333 B.C. he marched into Gordium, Phyrgia (that's in Turkey these days) with his army.

He came upon an ancient wagon, its yoke tied with an intricate tangle of knots. Local tradition held that the knot had been tied by Gordius the father of the famous King Midas and an oracle had declared that whoever untied the knot would one day rule all of Asia.

Naturally Alexander took up the challenge. He wrestled with it for some time to no avail. Standing back he declared that it made no difference how it was loosened, drew his sword and sliced open the knot to the immediate acclaim of his army. That night Gordium was battered with thunder and lightning that Alexander declared was a sign of approval from the gods.

He went on to conquer Egypt and most of Asia before his death at the age of 32. He died in the palace of Nebuchadnezzar II in Babylon which he planned to make his capital city. It is unclear if he fell ill with something like typhoid or whether he was poisoned. He was buried in a golden coffin filled with honey but his final resting place is now unknown.

The question of how the Gordian knot got on the ox-cart in the first place is unusual too. Many years before Alexander, the Phyrgians were without a king. Their oracle announced that the next man to enter the city driving an ox-cart should become their king. A peasant farmer called Gordius duly arrived with his cart and was proclaimed king with the city being named in his honour.

His son, King Midas, dedicated the cart to the gods and it stood in the palace grounds from that time until Alexander turned up, presumably tightening up the knot with weather over the years. Lucky that Midas never touched it, or it would have turned to gold.

Alexander was tutored by Aristotle until the age of 16. Perhaps it was he who suggested the smooth marketing move of calling him "The Great". Alexander founded twenty cities that bore his name, a sure way to get his name into the geography and history books, if not the dictionary.

Shakespeare referenced the story of the knot in his play "Henry V" and in modern times it is seen as a metaphor for seeing the simple solution to a problem.

Hamburger

A hamburger is a sandwich consisting of one or more cooked patties of meat inside a roll or bun. A staple of the fast food menu, there's always a joke to be had about the lack of ham in a hamburger but the reason is simple – the ham in hamburger relates to a river, not meat.

The hamburger is named after Hamburg, the second largest city in Germany. The burg part of Hamburg references a castle or fortified settlement while the ham part is from an Old High German word hamma meaning a bend in the river.

It's not entirely clear that the hamburger was first cooked in Hamburg, however. Descriptions of the dish entered newspapers from 1884 and various rivals claim the first invention but it wasn't until the 1904 St. Louis World Fair that hamburgers reached a large audience. It is likely that several chefs came up with the idea at around the same time. One version of the story links the invention to Hamburg, New York rather than Germany.

Following World War I, anti-German sentiment ran high so hamburgers were re-named Salisbury Steak for a time.

The McDonalds franchise began in 1940 and they now sell about 550 million hamburgers in the U.S. every year.

The navy has an abundance of amusing slang terms for food but one special hamburger is eponymous. The Barney Clark is a hamburger topped with a fried egg and it is named after the first man to receive an artificial heart transplant in 1982. The hearts are used typically as a stop-gap solution until a human heart is available for transplant.

By Hook or By Crook

This phrase means to use whatever means necessary to

achieve an objective.

There are several competing stories for its origins.

In medieval England there was a feudal custom allowing peasants to harvest dead wood from royal forests but only what they could pull down with a shepherd's crook or cut with a reaper's billhook. This was an important concession in a time when the crown owned huge tracts of forestry in the country and peasants rarely owned their own land. Hunting on the king's land would have landed you on the gallows but at least this way they could light a fire to warm their families. The combination of hook and crook allegedly gave us the phrase although it's hard to see that using a simple hand tool is the same as using whatever means are necessary.

One alternative story is eponymous and is popularly believed in Ireland to be the origin of the phrase. It is possible that the phrase had one root in England and a different one in Ireland.

The Irish legend goes that when Oliver Cromwell (1599-1658) was laying siege to Waterford city in 1649-1650 he claimed Waterford city would fall to his forces "by hook or by crook". The town could be entered by landing an army at either Hook Head with its famous ancient lighthouse or via Crook village on the opposite side of the channel. The problem with this story is that the phrase is used in English documents in the 1300s predating Cromwell's campaign to subdue Ireland.

A more likely tale, again eponymous and Irish, relates to an earlier English visitor to Irish shores – King Richard III (1452-1485). The voyage to Ireland from England could be perilous, depending on weather, and many ships sank. The two most extreme points on the southern Irish coast where they could harbour safely were Hook Head in County Wexford or Crookhaven in County Cork, further west. If they overshot the inlets between these two points they would be swept around to the Western coast of Ireland which was known to be treacherous and indeed dealt punishing blows to the Spanish Armada in the late 1500s because of their lack of charts and the wild weather. Therefore the Normans vowed to land by Hook or by Crook.

My own theory is that all three are correct. The feudal firewood custom would have been known to King Richard III and his nobles, thus leading to their vow to steer for Hook or Crook(haven). Such navigation advice was probably still in use by Cromwell's time so it's not surprising that he'd adopt the same approach to conquering the south coast. Cromwell and his army had a devastating effect on Ireland so it's understandable that his use of the phrase is the one that stuck in the collective memory.

Hunky Dory

Hunky dory is an expression meaning that everything is fine. Its spelling has varied widely over time with hunkey dorey being one of the earliest in print in an 1862 American song. By 1866 it was hunkee doree or hunky-dore.

That variation in spelling would seem to suggest that the expression was still only verbal slang. It hadn't been regularised. Hunkey was also used around that time to indicate someone or something being fit, healthy, and ready for action.

There's strong evidence to suggest that hunky dory originated in Japan rather than America and then travelled with mariners to American shores.

Commodore Matthew Perry (1794-1858) opened up trade to Japan in the 1850s by use of gunboat diplomacy and smart treaties. He is considered the father of the steam navy and fought hard to establish proper training academies for the U.S. navy.

By the 1860s (when hunky dory arrived in American English) there were frequent voyages between the two countries. Japanese has a term "honcho-dori" which translates as main street and as a result many cities have one.

American sailors would have known the word hunky and may have either substituted it or misheard honcho. There appears to have been honcho-dori or honki-dori streets in both Tokyo and Yokohama which had a large number of friendly young ladies residing there to provide solace to long-distance sailors.

Yokohama still has a street called Honcho-dori running from the city centre to the port area.

Hunky dory is the trade name of the most popular crinkle-cut flavoured crisp (chip for American readers) in Ireland. The producers sponsor the soccer stadium in Drogheda, Co. Louth which is called Hunky Dory Park.

India Pale Ale

With the rise of the hipster came the rise of craft beers, the more obscure the better. Many of them had IPA on the packaging but what did it mean?

IPA stands for India pale ale, a hoppy beer style within the category of pale ale. It was the answer to the problem of providing beer for the British Empire in the east. It was too hot to brew beer over there so colonial suppliers needed a beer that could survive the six month sea voyage to India.

A London brewer called George Hodgson created a strong, heavily-hopped beer called October Ale in his Bow brewery. The October Ale was usually aged before drinking. He sold his porters and beers to the East India Company whose headquarters lay a few miles downriver of his brewery.

The East India Company and the army became frustrated with Hodgson's quality so he tried unfermented beer with yeast added on arrival. He tried shipping beer concentrate that was diluted on arrival. His final effort was October Ale which he created to be aged like wine. He intended it to replace wine which was hard to come by thanks to years of wars with Napoleonic France.

In 1822 it survived the trip and actually improved on the way. IPAs gradually became paler and lighter after that point to eventually give us modern-style IPAs.

Over time the IPAs fell out of favour in Britain but they were revived thanks to craft brewing in America in the 1970s and made their way back to Britain in more recent times.

Magenta

This bright pink shade is best known to designers and artists. You will typically find it in a box of watercolours. Magenta is named for the town of that name in Lombardy, Italy.

On the 4th of June 1859 Napoleon faced General Franz Gyulai of Austria there and nearly 9,000 troops died. Their bones were gathered in an ossuary which still stands.

Meanwhile the very first red aniline dyes hit the market under the names fuchine or roseine. They were probably named to be like carmine, another dye, and to evoke the colours of fuchsia or roses. Unfortunately fuchine didn't sell. When the name was changed to magenta in honour of the battle, and the rather gruesome association with blood reds, it flew off the shelves. Gore outsells floristry apparently.

Manila Folders and Envelopes

Manila folders are those buff-coloured card folders made by simply folding a large piece of card in half. They typically hold loose document sheets. Manila envelopes are similar in size so they can hold unfolded documents. They often have a closure device that allows for re-use.

Manila folders were originally made from the fibres of the abaca plant which originated in the Philippines. The folders were first sold in the 1800s and they were stiffer than those we use today. The abaca plant (Musa Textilis in Latin) was also known as Manila Hemp or just manila after the capital city of the Philippines. It's not actually a relative of the hemp family, it's closer to a banana tree.

By 1921 America had established abaca plantations in Central America and later expanded production to cope with increased demand during World War II.

Abaca is no longer used to make manila folders but they are still manufactured in the yellowish-brown colour of the originals. The world's biggest producer of abaca is the Philippines. It is now used for rope, fibre arts, paper, and textiles.

Manila is an eponym but so are the Philippines. The islands were named for King Philip II of Spain.

Marathon

The 26 mile race known as a marathon is named for the Battle of Marathon in 490 B.C. between the citizens of

Athens and the Persian army. The race is named after the legendary run when the Greek soldier Pheidippides ran non-stop from the battlefield in Marathon to Athens to bring the glad tidings that the Greeks had won. Unfortunately the run was too much for him. He collapsed and died after delivering the news but the legend and the distance lived on. His run was 25 miles (40km) and that's the distance a marathon was up until the 1920s.

There's some debate about the details of the legend. Herodotus, the famous Greek historian of the period, mentions the run but says Pheidippides was a messenger who ran from Athens to Sparta asking for help and then ran back again with the answer which would have been a distance of 240km (150 miles), each way. Presumably *that* run wasn't non-stop. Herodotus doesn't mention a messenger from the Battle of Marathon but does say that the entire army marched back from it in a hurry as they feared a Persian naval raid against Athens which was undefended.

The Greeks were understandably worried as King Darius of Persia had sworn to burn Athens to the ground in response to an earlier battle. He even hired a servant to remind him of his vow three times a day before dinner. The Greek army arrived back in less than a day which may have given rise to the story of the messenger. Either way, those ancient Greeks were fast.

The first modern marathon was held in the 1896 Olympics in Athens, Greece. It was won by a Greek man named Spyridion Louis. The ancient Olympic Games (776 B.C.-393 A.D.) never included a long distance race.

In 1908 the distance of the Olympic marathon was changed to be 26 miles and 385 yards to allow the British royal family to view the start at Windsor Castle. Queen Alexandra had requested the marathon start from the lawn of the castle, possibly so the littlest royals could watch from their nursery window, and finish in front of the royal box at the Olympic stadium. This distance was agreed upon for all marathons from 1921.

Marathons were male only events until the 1970s in most countries and it only became a female Olympic sport in 1984. The race length has soared in popularity in recent years and there are more than 1,100 marathon events in the U.S. alone each year.

In 1960 Abebe Bikila of Ethiopia won the Olympic marathon barefoot.

The nutty marathon chocolate bar was available 1973-1981 but is now called a snickers.

Munro

A munro is a mountain which is at least 914m (3,000 feet) high, typically in Scotland. Qualifying mountains outside of Scotland, but in the British Isles, are called furth munros. The Scottish mountaineer Sir Hugh Thomas Munro (1856-1919) published a table of munros in the Scottish Mountaineering Club's journal in 1891 but sadly he died without climbing all of them, he missed two including the one nearest to his own home which he had been saving until last.

In the table of munros he listed 283 summits with a further 255 summits as subsidiary tops. He caused quite a stir as up to that time it had been thought there were only about 30 mountains of that height in the country.

The first to bag them all was Rev. A.E. Robertson (1870-1958) and he completed the task in 1901. His celebration on the final summit probably led to years of marital strife. He first kissed the cairn of rocks at the top and then kissed his wife.

The second to bag them all was also a clergyman, the Rev. Ronald Burn in 1923 and he also climbed all the subsidiary tops.

Thanks to an explosion of interest in hillwalking in the 1980s, many people now enjoy collecting the summits in their walks. Climbers who seek to walk all of them are called munro-baggers and those who manage them all are called compleaters or Munroists. The youngest compleater is Ben Fleetwood who finished his list in 2011 aged 10 years and 3 months.

The best known munro is Ben Nevis, the highest mountain in the British Isles.

Rugby

The sport of rugby, a fast game of kicking and running with an oval ball involving moves like line-outs, rucks, mauls, and scrums, is named for the private boys' school Rugby.

Popular legend has it that the game was created in 1823 when William Ellis Webb with a fine disregard for the rules of football (soccer) took the ball in his arms and ran with it. There's little proof this actually happened but it is so firmly entrenched in the minds of rugby players and supporters worldwide that when they came to name the Rugby World Cup trophy they called it after Webb. Webb played cricket, but not rugby, for Oxford University and became a clergyman.

Early forms of soccer had been played since the middle

ages, and probably even in Roman times as a game called harpastum. It often resembled a mob rather than a sport with the entire village on one side or the other. Each side struggled to kick an inflated pig's bladder through the town to markers to win.

Predictably the wildness of these games led them to be outlawed. In the period 1314-1527 nine European monarchs outlawed the playing of football and encouraged their subjects to practice their archery instead which was a nice useful skill for warfare. Youths continued to play football.

By 1750, the game of football, as played at the school in Rugby, allowed the handling of the ball and still involved huge numbers of players on each side, but nobody was allowed run with it in their hands towards the goal, at least until Webb presumably gave it a go. The introduction of running with ball in hand happened there sometime between 1820 and 1830 and was probably met with outrage on this "breaking" of the rules. However by 1841 it had become an essential part of the game. Rugby and soccer were different sports from that time.

The game, and its formal code of rules, came to be played at other private boys' schools and gradually crept into mainstream sporting life. By 1871 the Rugby Football Union was founded and more detailed rules drawn up. Later the sport spawned American football and Australian Rules football. In 1876 there was a schism, largely down to money and class issues, in the rugby world that resulted in rugby union and rugby league and eventual changes in rules on both sides.

Wasps, a well-known rugby union club, missed out on being a founding member of the Rugby Football Union because their representative went to the wrong pub for the meeting.

In 1995 rugby became a professional sport.

Many of the national sides in rugby union have nicknames – the Springboks (South Africa), All Blacks (New Zealand), les Bleus (France), the Wallabies (Australian), los Pumas (Argentina), the Eagles (U.S.A.), and the Dragons (Wales).

Serendipity

Serendipity means to find something you are not looking for by a fortunate chance and it is named after Sri Lanka.

The word was coined by Horace Walpole (1717-1797) in 1754 and he explained in a letter to his friend Horace Mann that he'd made a useful discovery in a Persian fairy tale "The Three Princes of Serendip" where the princes were wise enough to be constantly making accidental discoveries of things they were not actually seeking.

The concept of serendipity is rife in the field of invention and science – Alexander Fleming wasn't looking for penicillin in 1928, Percy Spencer accidentally devised the microwave oven in 1945 and Spencer Silver's post-it note was an experiment gone wrong. The idea of serendipity is vital in many creative pursuits also where errors push artists to new levels. Of course the ability to see a bridge or connection where another sees a mistake or hole is key to serendipity.

Serendip was the Persian name for Sri Lanka (formerly known as Ceylon). Sri Lanka belonged to the Kings of Kerala at one point and they were known as the Cheran kings. Dheep meant island so Cherandeep was the island of the Keralan kings to traders.

"The Three Princes of Serendip" dates back to 1302, at least. The king ensures his sons have the best education. When he offers to retire and give them the throne, each refuses. He sends them away to broaden their experience in life. On their travels they encounter various clues that they use, Sherlock Holmes-style, to deduce amazing levels of details about things they have never seen (such as a lame one-eyed camel ridden by a pregnant woman). They nearly end up in trouble for stealing the camel but luckily it turns up wandering in the desert at the perfect moment. Their adventures continue in this manner until they reach a happy ending.

In chapter three of Voltaire's novel "Zadig" there's an adaptation of the camel story involving a camel, a horse, and a dog which Zadig describes in huge detail. He clears himself of theft charges by explaining the mental processes that allow him to make the description so detailed. Edgar Allan Poe and Arthur Conan Doyle were probably inspired by "Zadig" and it is credited as being the jumping-off point for the detective fiction genre.

There are two related eponymous terms to serendipity. The first is zemblanity which means an unpleasant surprise and it is named for Nova Zembla, a cold barren island with many opposite features to Sri Lanka. Nova Zembla is a sparsely-populated Russian island in the Arctic ocean which has been used for nuclear bomb testing. Willem Barents (1550-1597) and his crew were stranded there while searching for the Northeast Passage. Willem, a Dutch cartographer and explorer, died on the return trip and the Barents Sea is named for him.

The second term is bahramdipity which is from the name of Bahram Gur who receives the three princes in "The Three Princes of Serendip" story. Bahram Gur (406-438) was the real life king of Persia and he features in many legends of war, love, and hunting. He is a key figure in Persian literature. Bahramdipity means the suppression of serendipitous discoveries by powerful individuals.

Stockholm Syndrome

Stockholm syndrome is a psychological phenomenon first described in 1973 where those captured or held hostage develop sympathy and other positive feelings towards their captors. It happens in approximately 8% of hostage victims according to FBI statistics.

The syndrome was first identified after a six day bank robbery at Norrmalmstorg, Stockholm, Sweden. The hostages became emotionally attached to the robbers, rejected help from the police, and defended their captors after their release.

The Norrmalmstorg robbery was the first criminal event covered live on Swedish television.

One of the men involved in the robbery, Clark Olofsson, had his conviction squashed by the court of appeal. He insisted he'd been trying to keep the hostages safe. He wasn't involved in the initial robbery but did have a long record of similar crimes. After his release he met with one of the hostages many times and their families became friends.

A similar, but reverse, effect is Lima syndrome where the captor develops sympathy for their captive. It was named after an attack on the Japanese embassy in Lima, Peru in 1996. A militant movement took hundreds of people hostage at an embassy party but within a few hours released them owing to developing sympathy for them.

Times Square

Times Square, the flashy New York midtown square beloved of directors and tourists alike, wasn't always called Times Square. In 1900 it was Longacre Square and it was a boring intersection far away from thriving Lower Manhattan.

Then subway pioneer August Belmont and New York Times publisher Adolph Ochs made a deal. Belmont was heading up construction of the city's first subway line from lower Manhattan to the Upper West Side and Harlem. He realised a commercial hub on 42nd Street would draw passengers to the route. He approached Ochs and suggested moving the New York Times operations to the intersection of Broadway and 42nd Street to give Ochs a double win — a handy subway station for newspaper distribution around the city and sales to subway commuters right outside their headquarters.

Belmont sweetened the deal by getting Mayor George B. McClellan Junior to rename the square in honour of the newspaper. Ochs couldn't resist. In the winter of 1904-1905 the subway and the newspaper opened in the newly renamed square. To celebrate the New York Times hosted a New Year's Eve party in 1904 with fireworks from its skyscraper's roof. By 1907 the fireworks were too dangerous as the area had become more built up, so the paper created a 700lb wood and iron ball to be lowered from the top of their building at midnight.

The New York Times left the square for 8th Avenue in 1960 but the tradition continues with a Waterford Crystal ball every New Year's Eve. Around a million people gather to watch it at the square named for a newspaper. The ball drop did not happen in 1942 and 1943 due to wartime lighting restrictions. A moment's silence was observed at midnight instead.

If you're visiting New York and it's not New Year's Eve you can see the "ball drop" at the Times Square Museum every twenty minutes. Time flies at Times Square.

Times Square draws an estimated 50 million visitors every year.

The electronic news ticker in Times Square is now operated by Reuters News Agency, not the New York Times.

Timbuktu and Tipperary

Timbuktu is used as a word for an exotic and remote location. Many think it is a legendary or fictional place but it does exist and it has a rich history. It's on the edge of the Sahara desert in the Republic of Mali.

Timbuktu was founded by the Tuareg people. A nomadic people, they roamed the desert with their camels and herds during the rainy season and settled at Timbuktu, near the River Niger (that gives us Nigeria) during the dry season. When the desert became green they left their heavier belongings with an older woman, called Timbuktu, while they travelled with the herds. The name of the town came from this formidable woman.

From the 11th century Timbuktu's location meant it became where the camel met the canoe, with trade moving from the desert and onto the river. It became a trading point for goods from North Africa, West Africa, and the Mediterranean.

By the 12th century the city had a university and was a centre for Islamic learning with a thriving book copying industry. One scholar of the time had his "small" library of 1,600 books plundered. Locals said that gold came from the south, salt from the north, and divine knowledge from Timbuktu.

Despite several conquests, the city thrived until the Moroccan army invaded in 1591. They sacked the city, plundered the wealth, burned the libraries, and put to death many of the scholars. In 1893 Timbuktu was colonised by the French until they granted Mali independence in 1960.

Tipperary is also famously a place that is a "long way from here". Tipperary is a county in Ireland - like a state in America only much smaller. It's a lovely green part of the country but it's not a particularly long way from anywhere in Ireland.

Any journey's length depends on the starting point however and the famous song "It's a Long, Long Way to Tipperary" is set in London which would have involved a long journey in the early 1900s by rail, boat, and cart. The song became popular with World War I troops. The famous Irish tenor John McCormack recorded it in 1914 and the title passed into phrase forever.

The song was written by Jack Judge (1872-1938) and Henry James Williams (1873-1924) in 1912 for a five shilling bet. The next night Jack Judge performed it in a music hall.

Jack Judge's grandparents were from Tipperary.

The song became a running gag in the Snoopy cartoons featuring Snoopy as a World War I flying ace.

Welcome signs in Tipperary include the words "you've come a long way".

Getting Your Name into the Atlas

Atlases are less discerning than dictionaries. Explorers and cartographers regularly named whatever they'd discovered after themselves, their monarch, or their patron although I prefer the place-names that translate from the local language into things like "it's a mountain, you idiot" because naming rights really should go to the native people.

If you're finding the dictionary thing too difficult then it's time to found a town, find a new river, or discover a remote spot.

Queen Elizabeth I was probably the most successful monarch in this regard. Known as the Virgin Queen, she ruled during a major era of exploration by her subjects and the atlas is littered with Virginia towns, cities, and falls. Queen Victoria, and her consort Prince Albert, also did well in this regard. Saints get an unfair advantage in this game as towns were often named for a local patron saint.

Other eponymous cities and countries include; Constantinople (Istanbul now), Washington, Columbia, America, Bolivia, the Cook Islands, the Philippines, Rhodesia (now Zambia and Zimbabwe), Alice Springs, Alberta, Alexandria, Athens (for Athena, goddess of wisdom), Wellington, Lincoln, Pittsburgh, and Livingstone.

Space precludes a full list, but you'll find a good resource at
https://en.wikipedia.org/wiki/List_of_places_named_after_people.

Conclusion

Place names galore have entered the English language with help from criminals, watercolour paints, music hall bets, subway entrepreneurs, slave ships, and tea shops. Entering the dictionary via a town legend or an atlas entry may be the easiest method.

7
Be a Greek, or a God,
or Preferably Both

The English language would be sparse indeed if we removed all the words with Greek roots. This is equally true when eponyms are considered. Those Greeks, especially their pantheon of gods and goddesses, fuelled the dictionary for hundreds of years. Once you add in Roman gods and the Egyptians your dictionary is overflowing.

With classical studies and learning Greek and Latin being less popular pursuits in recent years some of the following stories may be news to you. We sometimes forget how intertwined Greek and Latin are with the English language.

Becoming a god to get a spot in the dictionary is a somewhat extreme route to fame but imagine how much fun you could have with a lightning bolt.

Academy

Plato's academy was a pleasure garden in suburban Athens where Plato taught his followers. He founded it in 387 B.C. and it was the first higher learning institution in the Western World. Aristotle studied there before founding his own school, the Lyceum.

The site of the academy had been sacred to Athena, the Greek goddess of wisdom, since the Bronze age and it held a grove of sacred olive trees. Even when the Spartans conquered the area they refused to ravage these groves, although sadly the Romans chopped them to build siege engines in 86 B.C.. Torch-lit races and funeral games took place there and the road to the academy was lined with the gravestones of Athenians.

Plato's academy, founded in this special place, was free to attend and women were amongst the students. The subjects, informally taught, included mathematics, philosophy, and astronomy with frequent debates and lectures by Plato.

The academy was named for the mythical Greek hero Akademos who had owned the land where the olive grove and later the academy was established. He was renowned for saving the city of Athens due to yet another disaster caused by Helen of Troy. This was before the Trojan War and this time it wasn't her fault.

King Theseus, the slayer of the minotaur and the ruler of Athens was now 50 and widowed. He abducted Helen, then aged only 12. Her twin demi-god brothers Castor and Pollux threatened to destroy Athens to liberate their young sister. Akademos knew where she was hidden and revealed the location to the twins thus saving Athens.

When he died he was buried in the olive grove on his land which was long-dedicated to Athena.

Raphael's famous fresco "The School of Athens" on the walls of the Vatican Museum depicts the students at Plato's academy.

The site of the academy was rediscovered in the 20th century and is now a free museum.

Ammonia

Ammonia is a colourless, poisonous, soluble gas. Its name comes from the Latin sal ammoniacus. Ammoniac is a salt or resin thought to come from an area in Libya near the temple of the Egyptian god Ammon.

Ammonia was first obtained in its pure form in 1774 by English chemist and clergyman Joseph Priestley (1733-1804) by heating sal ammoniac with slack lime (calcium hydroxide). He called it alkaline air but in 1787 it got its official name – ammoniac – from the sal ammoniac ingredient.

Ammonia is used in the production of nylon, as smelling salts for fainting fits, in industrial refrigeration units, fertilisers, and explosives.

Priestley also discovered oxygen, sulphur dioxide, and invented soda water which he hoped would be a cure for scurvy. Despite a stutter due to illness as a child, he learned Greek, Latin, Hebrew, French, Italian, German, Aramaic, and Arabic.

Ammon, also known as Amum-Ra, was the king of the Egyptian gods and was also worshipped in Libya, Greek, and Nubia (now Northern Sudan). He was the patron god of Thebes as early as 2,000 B.C.. When Thebes became the Egyptian capital city, his importance rose and he was prayed to as protector of the road and seen as giving justice to the poor. Over time he was merged with other gods like Ra (sun god) and Min (a ram-like fertility god). He emerged as a virtual super-god with characteristics of a solar god, creator god, and fertility god. However from 1,000 B.C. his worship began to decline.

Ammon's name was incorporated in Tutankhamun's which translates as "the living image of Amun".

The oracles of Ammon in Libya were widely respected. Alexander the Great travelled there during his occupation of Egypt and was declared a son of Amun by the oracle. Thereafter he considered himself divine. Alexander had a healthy ego.

Ammonites, the spiral fossil shells of extinct cephalopods, are named for Ammon's ram's horns.

Arachnid

Arachnids are the eight-legged invertebrate class which includes spiders, scorpions, ticks, and mites.

They are named for Arachne, a girl from Lydia, who was so skilled at weaving and needlecraft that even the nymphs came to watch her work. Some suggested that she had been taught by the goddess Athena herself but this she denied saying that Athena could come and test her skill against her if she dared.

Athena, the goddess of wisdom, craft, and war, wasn't one to shirk a challenge. Arachne, although she paled when the goddess revealed herself from her old woman disguise, agreed to the contest.

They each stood at their loom. Athena wove a scene of her contest with Poseidon. All four corners were adorned with scenes depicting the displeasure of the gods with presumptuous mortals who challenged their power. The threat was clear.

Arachne filled her weaving with scenes of the gods' failings and weaknesses, an equally clear message.

Athena's rage boiled over. She rent Arachne's weaving from the frame and touched the mortal's forehead, making her feel guilt and shame for dishonouring the gods. Arachne ran out and hanged herself.

Athena was moved to pity when she saw the girl suspended by the rope. She brought her back to life but transformed her into a spider and commanded her, and her descendants, to hang in all future times. To this day the spider weaves beautiful webs and hangs from her own thread.

Atlas

{with thanks to Rick Ellrod at https://rickellrod.com/}

According to Greek legends the titans, a race of giants, ruled the earth before Zeus and the Greek gods. Zeus battled them and the titans lost. Each was punished and the one called Atlas was condemned to support the heavens upon his shoulders for eternity.

Atlas nearly escaped his task when he met Hercules. Hercules was seeking golden apples from Hera's garden, as part of his famous ten labours. Atlas' daughters tended the garden and Hercules begged his aid. Atlas agreed to help him if he would hold the skies for a time. Hercules agreed, proud of his own great strength, but he was no titan. By the time Atlas returned, Hercules knew he would be crushed if he continued this particular task.

When Atlas saw Hercules under the heavenly globe he decided to walk away and leave him there. Hercules declared the sky was uncomfortable, asking Atlas to take it for a moment while he adjusted a pad on his shoulders. Atlas, unthinking, took it and Hercules ran away with the apples. Atlas continued his allotted task until he turned into the Atlas Mountains in northwest Africa.

In some versions of the legend Atlas wasn't a titan but a King of Mauretania and an expert astronomer.

In the late 16th century Geradus Mercator compiled a book of maps and called it an atlas. He included the story of Atlas and a drawing of him on the title page of the collection as the astronomer king. Ever since then books of maps have been called atlases.

The Atlantic Ocean means "sea of Atlas" and Atlantis means "island of Atlas" perhaps because Atlas was rumoured to stand, still holding the skies, in the west.

Cassandra

To be a cassandra is to predict bad things and never be believed. It reaches English from the Greek tales of the Trojan War.

Cassandra was the beautiful daughter of Priam, the King of Troy. The god Apollo fell in love with her and she gained the gift of prophecy when one of his temple snakes licked her ears. She refused his advances and he cursed her that she would see the future but nobody would believe her predictions.

Cassandra foresaw the Trojan War, warning Paris not to abduct Helen. Later she foresaw the fall of Troy. When the Trojans found the huge wooden horse outside their gates she warned that the Greeks would destroy them if they brought it inside the city's walls. She originated the phrase "beware Greeks bearing gifts".

Nobody in Troy believed her. They pulled the horse inside and the concealed Greeks conquered Troy. Cassandra tried to find shelter in the temple of Athena but was brought as a spoil of war to Agamemnon who took her back to Greece. She predicted his doom too. She and he were murdered by his wife Clytemnestra and her lover Aegisthus.

Legend says that Cassandra was sent to the Elysian Fields after her death thanks to her lifelong dedication to the gods. The fields were separate to the realm of Hades. They were a blessed spot where the righteous and heroic would live a happy afterlife.

The cassandra syndrome, named by French philosopher Gaston Bachelard in 1949, applies when valid alarms are disbelieved particularly in the fields of science and politics.

Cereal

Cereal is named, via the Latin word cerealis, for Ceres the Roman goddesses of harvest and agriculture, who is often associated with the earlier Greek goddess, Demeter. Ceres' name was used as a synonym for grain and bread from Roman times onwards.

Ceres' main festival was Ceriales, a seven day event in April including horse races, plays, and games. Her followers sacrificed pigs to her, particularly at funerals and marriages, as she was linked to life transitions - from life to death or girlhood to womanhood.

The dwarf planet Ceres, discovered in 1801, is named for this goddess.

Ceres appears as a character in "The Tempest" by William Shakespeare.

Colossal

The seven wonders of the ancient world gave us two words – colossal and mausoleum (discussed below). Colossal comes from the Colossus at Rhodes.

The island of Rhodes was an important economic hub in the ancient world thanks to its strategic position at the meeting of the Aegean and Mediterranean seas. The main town, also called Rhodes, was built to take advantage of the island's best natural harbour. The island was conquered several times - by King Mausolos (see mausoleum below) in 357 B.C., the Persians in 340 B.C., and Alexander the Great in 332 B.C..

Alexander's huge kingdom was divided in three by his generals after his early death and Rhodes went to Ptolemy, angering another general, Demetrius, who proceeded to bring an army of 40,000 men to attack the island, more than the island's entire population.

Demetrius would have to conquer Rhodes' high walls, however. His first giant siege tower toppled in a storm. His second mired in the mud created by clever islanders who flooded a ditch outside the walls. Finally troops arrived from Egypt to support the defenders and Demetrius retreated.

The islanders decided to celebrate their victory with a giant statue to their patron sun god Helios using the siege tower for scaffolding and the melted down bronze war machines for the statue's skin. Construction of the Colossus at Rhodes took 12 years. When finished, it stood 110 feet high on a fifty foot pedestal near the entrance to their harbour.

Despite popular, and much later, paintings, the statue stood to one side of the harbour in classic Greek statue pose, not spanning the entrance to the harbour. Even Shakespeare got that one wrong. It may have had a crown of sun rays on its head in honour of Helios.

The sculptor was Chares of Lindos, a local who had fought in the defence of the city. He died before the statue was complete. The statue lasted for just 56 years until an earthquake in 226 B.C. caused large chunks to fall off the inner framework. King Ptolemy III of Egypt offered to help pay for its restoration but the people of Rhodes feared they had angered Helios thanks to advice from the Oracle at Delphi, and refused to repair it.

In the 7th century Arab invaders broke up the remains of the statue for scrap metal and it took 900 camels to take it away.

The Statue of Liberty in New York harbour is sometimes called The Modern Colossus and is the same height as the ancient one.

In the "Game of Thrones" books and TV series the city of Bravos is depicted with a colossus bestriding the entrance to its port, complete with defenders inside the torso.

Erotic

Eros was the Greek god of love and passionate desire hence the giving of his name to all things erotic.

His randomly-aimed arrows loosened the limbs and weakened the mind. He was a handsome, winged youth crowed with flowers, usually roses, so that explains how florists earn their money on the 14th of February.

In some stories he has a younger brother, Anteros, who was the avenger of unrequited love.

Eros could be seen as a malignant force with his forcing of random attractions so it is some comfort to discover that he was a victim of love too. He married Psyche against his mother Aphrodite's wishes. Their love encountered difficulties afterwards which are explained in Psyche's section below.

When Eros was adopted into the Roman gods he transformed into a rather cheeky and rotund baby and renamed Cupid.

Hypnosis

Like mesmerism, hypnosis is an eponym. Hypnos was the Greek god of sleep. Appropriately enough he was the son of Nyx, the goddess of night, and Erebus, the god of darkness. He had a twin brother, Thanatos, Death.

He wasn't the most active of gods. He spent his time on a soft couch by the River Lethe whose waters brought oblivion and forgetfulness and whose banks were planted with poppies.

His sons joined the family business. Morpheus brought the dreams of men, Icelus brought the dreams of animals and Phantasus brought dreams of inanimate things and was known for creating illusions. He was attended by Aergia, the goddess of sloth.

Hypnosis and hypnotic come from his name but so too does insomnia as his Roman name was Somnus.

Iris

The iris can be a flower or the coloured part of an eye. Both types of irises are named for Iris, the Greek goddess of the rainbow.

Iris was the messenger of Hera, queen of the gods. She was the personification of the rainbow and iris means rainbow in Greek.

Iris travelled along her rainbow with the speed of the wind to bring messages to earth. She had golden wings to help her on her way. It's not surprising that she travelled with the speed of the wind as she married Zephyrus, the god of the west wind.

By the command of Zeus she carried a jug of water from the River Styx, the river souls cross to enter the realm of Hades. She used this to put to sleep those who perjure themselves.

The word iridescence comes from her name.

The element iridium is named for her.

Mausoleum

A mausoleum is a grand, stately tomb and it comes to us from King Mausolus, the ruler of Haliacarnassus in Asia Minor. He ruled for 24 years, ruling Rhodes for a short while. He greatly admired the Greek way of life and encouraged Greek democratic traditions.

When he died in 353 B.C. his widow Artemisia built a magnificent tomb at Haliacarnassus for him. It was a raised temple made of white marble in a mixture of Greek and Egyptian styles. She adorned it with statues and a 24-level stepped pyramid roof. Set on a hill overlooking their capital city, the tomb was the work of several famous architects and sculptors. A row of stone lions guarded the entrance stairway.

Soon after construction started the Rhodians heard of the king's death and decided to attack his kingdom. Queen Artemisia hid her own fleet and let the Rhodians land. Then her fleet attacked by surprise and took the Rhodian fleet easily. They sailed it back to Rhodes where they captured the city whose residents thought they were welcoming back their own fleet. The rebellion was defeated.

Sadly Artemisia only lived for two years after her husband's death and was buried with him in the unfinished tomb. The artists working on it decided to finish the tomb regardless of the death of both their patrons as a memorial to the sculptors' art.

The tomb stood as one of the seven wonders of the ancient world for 17 centuries, even above the eventual ruins of the city of Haliacarnassus, until it was destroyed by an earthquake in the 13th century.

The base of the tomb was plundered by Crusaders in 1522 to strengthen the castle at Haliacarnassus (Bodrum in modern Turkey). Some of the marble can still be seen there. Some of the sculptures were rescued and put on display in the castle. In the 1800s the British ambassador retrieved several of them and they are now on display in the British Museum. Later, thanks to some excellent detective work and excavation by Charles Thomas Newton in 1846 the remains of the sculpture of the king and queen from the rooftop were retrieved and these too are on display in the museum.

Only one of the seven wonders still exists – the great pyramid at Giza.

Mentor

A mentor is a wise and trusted advisor and it comes to us from Homer's "Odyssey".

Mentor was Odysseus' loyal friend, an older man who was left behind in Ithaca to run Odysseus' lands and guide his son Telemachus when Odysseus had sailed for war at Troy. Mentor's identity was assumed by Athena when she wanted to influence Telemachus and when she accompanied Telemachus in his search for his long-absent father.

Morphine and Morpheus

Morphine is a pain medication of the opiate family which is found naturally in various plants and animals but is most commonly produced from the opium poppy. It acts directly on the nervous system to ease chronic and acute pain. Unfortunately it has several serious side effects such as addiction, drowsiness, and withdrawal issues.

Morphine was first isolated by Friedrich Sertürner in 1804 and he named if after Morpheus, the Greek god of dreams because it made patients sleepy.

Narcissism

To be a narcissist one must possess an excessive love for oneself.

Narcissus was the son of a river god and nymph. He was loved by the god Apollo due to his extraordinary beauty. Men and women alike were attracted to him.

When a young man called Aminias fell in love with him, teenaged Narcissus spurned his advances and Aminias killed himself praying to the gods that Narcissus would be given a lesson for the pain he had caused.

When Narcissus was sixteen he was walking in the woods when a nymph called Echo saw him, fell madly in love, and began to follow him.

He sensed her presence and asked "Who's there?" but she merely repeated "Who's there?". Finally she showed herself and tried to embrace the boy but he told her to leave him alone. She was heartbroken and spent the rest of life in the glens until nothing but an echo of sound remained of her.

Nemesis (see below), the goddess of revenge, heard the tale and decided to punish the boy by making him love only his own reflection. He saw himself in the river and couldn't tear himself away, gradually fading from life and being transformed into the flower of his name which often grows by water, nodding at its own reflection.

According to one version of the legend Narcissus is still admiring himself in the Underworld, looking at the waters of the River Styx.

A related ancient myth is that of Pygmalion – a sculptor who fell in love with a statue he had carved.

Nemesis

Nemesis was the Greek goddess of vengeance and retribution. She punished human arrogance, also known as hubris.

She was considered to be remorseless and often appeared in Greek drama to cause suffering to the protagonist. According to an early Greek poet, Hesiod, she was the daughter of night. In art she is portrayed as a winged goddess with a whip or dagger in her hand. She rode in a chariot pulled by griffins.

She punished Narcissus, that vain young man, by condemning him to fall in love with his own reflection.

In another myth she created eggs from which hatched twins. The first pair was Helen of Troy and

Clytemenestra, the second set was the Dioscuri.

Helen of Troy caused the Trojan Wars and deaths of thousands while Clytemenestra, and her lover, murdered her husband Agamemnon when he returned from the Trojan War. It might be argued that Clytemenestra had some cause for the murder as Agamemnon had killed her first husband and taken her by force to be his wife. Plus he sacrificed their daughter Iphigenia to appease the wrath of the god Artemis before leaving for a ten year war.

The Dioscuri were Castor and Pollux. They had an eventful life and had a hand in causing the Trojan War too. When Castor was mortally wounded, Pollux asked that half his immortality be transferred to his twin, for somehow Pollux was a demigod son of Zeus while Castor had a mortal father. They were transformed into the constellation Gemini and were able to travel between Olympus and Hades.

The annual festival of Nemesis was held in Athens to avert the revenge of the dead on the living.

Oedipus Complex

Sigmund Freud (1856-1939) named this concept of a son's love for his mother and jealousy or hate towards his father after Oedipus but actually that wasn't what drove the original Oedipus.

Oedipus was the King of Thebes who accidentally killed his father and then married his mother. In some versions of the tale his mother killed herself when she realised their mistake.

When Laius, the King of Thebes, visited the oracle, they warned him his son would slay him. His wife duly gave birth to a boy and he had him exposed on the mountainside. The ancient Greeks were tough parents.

A shepherd took pity on the child and later the boy was adopted by King Polybus of Corinth. When he grew to manhood he too visited the oracle and learned of his destiny to kill his father. He vowed never to return to Corinth, thinking that Polybus was his true father.

On his travels he encountered his real father who provoked a quarrel and Oedipus killed him. When he arrived in Thebes it was being plagued by the Sphinx but Oedipus correctly solved its riddle and the Sphinx killed itself. His reward was the hand of Jocasta, his birth mother, and the throne to which he was an unknowing heir.

With a dysfunctional family history like that it is little wonder that Freud was drawn to the tale and used it to illustrate the struggle for alpha-male spot within a family unit.

Panic

Panic is a feeling of sudden terror and is named for the god Pan.

Pan was the Greek god of nature, the wild, and hunting. He is depicted in art as having a human body with goat legs and horns on his head. His companions were the wood-nymphs. He liked to chase them to seduce them but was always turned down due to his ugly appearance. His Roman god equivalent was Faunus.

There were no temples erected to Pan. He was worshipped in natural settings.

He had a wicked sense of humour and enjoyed pulling jump-scares on passersby. His voice was so frightening that it was said to cause panic in any who heard it. He was also considered the source of unearthly woodland noises at night that caused panic in travellers.

He, of course, also gives us the musical instrument called the syrinx, popularly known as pan-pipes. The instrument is named for a beautiful nymph of the same name who Pan desired. She ran away and was disguised by her sisters as a reed. When the wind blew across the reed it produced a beguiling melody. Pan, not knowing which reed was Syrinx, took several of them and joining them together in decreasing length he created the musical instrument.

Phobia

Until recent times people simply had fears. Spiders, heights, dogs, or buttons, the causes were various but now these all have individual phobia names, often created with a nod to some Latin. However phobia itself is of Greek origin.

Phobos was the Greek personification of fear. He was the son of Ares, the god of war, and would accompany his father into battle along with Eris, the goddess of discord, and Deimos, the god of terror. They really weren't a family you'd invite over for a barbeque.

Soldiers often made blood sacrifices to Phobos on battlefields to gain his favour. Heroes displayed his likeness, complete with his lion-head, on their shields.

The planet Mars has a satellite moon called Phobos named in his honour. Its smaller moon is called Deimos after his brother god.

Phobos' Roman equivalent was Timor who probably gives us the words timid and timorous as timere is Latin for "to fear".

Planets

All the planets in our solar system, except for Earth, are named for gods. This time the Romans beat the Greeks to it.

Mercury

Named after the messenger of the Roman gods because it appeared to move so swiftly.

Venus

Named after the Roman goddess of love because it shines so brightly. It is the brightest object in our night sky apart from the moon. Several other cultures also named the planet after their own gods of love or war.

Mars

Named for the Roman god of war because its red colour reminded them of blood and battle. The Egyptians named it Her Desher which means "the red one".

Jupiter

Named for the Roman king of the gods. As the largest planet in the system it was seen as the boss.

Saturn

Named for the father of Jupiter. Saturn was also the god of agriculture and harvest. Saturn had overthrown his own father, Uranus, to get the top spot and was in turn overthrown by Jupiter.

Uranus

Couldn't be seen without a telescope so it wasn't named by the Romans. It was discovered in 1781 by Sir William Herschel who named it Georgium Sidus in honour of King George III of England but others called it Herschel after its discoverer. Uranus, the father of Saturn, was suggested by astronomer Johann Bode and by the mid

1800s it had been generally accepted.

Neptune

Originally believed to be a star. John Couch Adams and Urban Le Verrier calculated its location. Johann Galle who discovered the planet in 1846 thanks to their calculations wanted to name it Verrier in their honour but other astronomers objected. Other names were suggested; such as Janus and Oceanus. By the end of the year Neptune, the Roman god of the seas, was settled upon which is appropriate as the planet is a bright sea blue. Neptune's astronomical symbol is a stylised version of Neptune's trident.

Earth

The only planet in our system not named for a god. Its name is based on Old German and Old English words for "ground" and hence is not an eponym.

Pluto

Pluto is now classified as a dwarf planet and was also named for a god, this time by an eleven year old girl. Pluto was discovered in 1930 by 23 year old Clyde

Tombaugh at Lowell Observatory. The observatory had the right to name the planet and they opened it to suggestions from the public. They got more than a thousand in return.

Pluto, the Roman god of the underworld and judge of the dead, was suggested by eleven year old Venetia Burney (1918-2009) in conversation with her grandfather Falconer Madan, a former librarian at the Bodleian in Oxford. He passed it on to an astronomy professor who told the Lowell team. Her suggestion won the selection committee's vote unanimously and her grandfather rewarded her with £5 (£300 sterling in modern terms).

Later that year Walt Disney was inspired by it to name Mickey Mouse's dog.

Several elements are named for planets – plutonium, uranium, and neptunium.

There are 67 known moons of Jupiter, the best known being the four discovered by Galileo Galilei – Ganymede, Callisto, Io, and Europa. From the end of the 19th century dozens of smaller Jovian moons have been discovered and they've been named for lovers, conquests, or daughters of Jupiter or Zeus (his Greek equivalent).

Platonic

A platonic relationship is one between a man and a woman which does not involve romantic emotions and interactions.

This form of spiritual or intellectual love was first described by the Greek philosopher Plato (c.427-347 B.C.) originally with reference to the pure love Socrates had for his young male students.

Plato's real name was Aristocles. Plato was a nickname referring to his broad shoulders.

He was born in to a wealthy, noble Athenian family. He was originally an athlete and poet but became a follower of Socrates. After Socrates was condemned to drink hemlock as death penalty for impiety and the corruption of youth in 399 B.C., Plato travelled widely for twelve years.

He founded his famous Academy (see above) in Athens on his return. He taught philosophy, mathematics, and government there.

Plato's most famous pupil was Aristotle. Together with Socrates, these three laid the core foundations of Western philosophy and science.

One legend says that when Plato was an infant, bees

landed on his lips while he was sleeping as a sign of the sweetness of his lecturing style later in his life.

There's some debate about how Plato, then in his eighties, died. Either it was quietly in his sleep or while attending a wedding.

Psychic or Psychotic

Psyche was the Greek goddess of the soul. It is from her name that we get psychology, psychotic, and psychic.

She was originally a mortal of great beauty. She roused the wrath of Aphrodite when men turned their worship from the goddess to the girl. Aphrodite commanded Eros, the Greek god of love, to make Psyche fall in love with a hideous man but when Eros met the girl he fell for her and whisked her away to his palace.

There he came to her only during the hours of darkness, to hide his true identity. He made her promise to never gaze upon his face but Psyche's sisters were jealous. They declared she was being visited by a horrible monster each night. Finally she lit an oil lamp during the night to view his face and was amazed to find the handsome god in her bed. A drop of the oil fell on him. He woke and stormed out.

Psyche searched the world for her lost love, going to the temple of each god in turn. Finally she entered the temple of Aphrodite who, still jealous of her loveliness, set her a near impossible collection of tasks which culminated in a visit to the Underworld.

Psyche, unknowingly, was aided by Eros in each of these tasks until she won over Aphrodite and having proven herself worthy she was made immortal. Then she was reunited with Eros and all the gods attended their wedding.

The daughter of Eros (love) and Psyche (soul) was Hedone – the goddess of pleasure – whose name gives us hedonism.

The fairy tale Beauty and the Beast is a re-telling of the Psyche and Eros story.

Python

A python is a large non-venomous snake that squeezes its victims. The python is named for the monstrous serpent called Python in Greek mythology.

The dragon Python lived at Delphi, which at that time was dedicated to the titan goddess Gaia (the earth mother). Greeks regarded Delphi as the centre of the earth and this was represented by a special navel stone called the omphalos which Python guarded.

When Zeus, who had serious fidelity issues, slept with the goddess Leto to father the twins Apollo and Artemis his wife Hera was furious. She ordered Python to hunt Leto so she couldn't give birth anywhere the sun shone. Leto finally settled on the newly formed island of Delos where she had her children. Apollo, as he grew up, vowed to take revenge on Python and in due course killed the serpent with his bow.

It was after killing Python that Apollo established his famous Oracle at Delphi who could see the future.

Zeus ordered Apollo to redeem himself for such sacrilege so he founded the Pythian Games. These were held two years after each Olympic games and included athletics, horse racing, art, and dance at Apollo's temple in Delphi. The winners were awarded bay laurel wreaths which were sacred to Apollo. The ancient stadium is still there.

The famous comedy group Monty Python were *not* named after this Greek dragon. The BBC wanted it to be "John Cleese's Flying Circus" because he was the best known of them but they wanted a nonsensical name and were in a rush. John Cleese suggested something slithery like a python for a surname and Eric Idle said Monty would be a good British drunken stereotype.

Stentorian

Someone who speaks in especially loud tones is stentorian. This style of speech is known to be booming and powerful.

Stentor was the herald during the Trojan War. Homer claims Stentor's voice was as loud as fifty men's voices. Stentor came to a sad end, dying when he lost a contest with Hermes, the herald of the gods.

Alexander the Great innovated a system of sound signals using a giant speaking trumpet called a stentorophonic tube. It was one of the scientific wonders of the ancient world and it could send the sound of a human voice for a dozen miles. There's a picture of one in the Vatican museum.

Stentor Music, a company established in the U.K. in 1895, specialises in making stringed instruments for students of music, presumably very loud ones.

Thespian

A thespian is another name for an actor or actress. It can be used as an adjective to describe anything related to drama and theatre. A thespian is also a citizen of the ancient Greek city state of Thespiae.

The 6th century B.C. Greek poet Thespis founded Greek tragic drama. Up to that point all drama was performed by the chorus but he introduced an actor to represent a historic or legendary figure. He is credited as being the first person to ever appear as a character in a play.

This new style of drama was called tragedy. In 534 B.C. a competition was held in Athens to find the best tragedy and he won. He then proceeded to tour the country with his plays, carrying his costumes, masks, and props in a horse-drawn wagon.

The touring company of the Greek national theatre, established in 1939, is called The Wagon of Thespis in his honour.

Titan

Titan or titanic is used to describe something or someone as being extremely large, for example the ill-fated ship the Titanic.

The titans were the twelve primeval gigantic Greek gods and goddesses who were the children of Uranus (the sky) and Gaia (the earth). There were six titans - Oceanus, Coeus, Crius, Hyperion, Japetus, and Cronus, plus six titanesses - Thea, Rhea, Themis, Mnemosyne, Phoebe, and Tethys.

The youngest titan, Cronus, became leader when he overthrew his father in the ten year war of the titans which was called the Titanomachy. In turn he was overthrown by Zeus who founded the Mount Olympus Greek gods.

The titans lived on Mount Othrys in northeastern Greece and were deities endowed with incredible strength.

Most of the titans were imprisoned in Tartarus after the Titanomachy ended. This lovely spot is the deepest part of the underworld where the most evil beings are cast to be tortured for all eternity.

Saturn's largest moon is called Titan.

The titans have spawned many pop culture references

and are a popular choice for naming sports teams.

Volcano

These erupting mountains are named for Vulcan, the Roman god of fire and metalworking. The only active volcano known to the ancients was Mount Etna in Sicily. They believed this was where Vulcan and the cyclopes forged Jupiter's thunderbolts.

Vulcan was the son of Jupiter and Juno. He was born ugly and his understanding mother tried to throw him off a cliff but he survived. Then she told him to go and live in a volcano for the rest of his life.

While there he became a talented blacksmith and made all the thrones for the gods including one that trapped his mother for three days unable to move, eat, or sleep. Finally Jupiter promised Vulcan a wife if he would release Juno from the trap. He did and was rewarded with Venus.

He then built a new smithy under Mourt Etna. Unfortunately Venus struggled to be faithful to her talented spouse. Each time he discovered her betrayal he would express his anger on his anvil, driving sparks and smoke to erupt from Etna.

Vulcan's festival, the Vulcanalia, was celebrated on the 23rd of August. The people would build bonfires and throw in small fish and animals as sacrifice to avert harmful summer wildfires.

Vulcanise

Vulcanisation is a chemical process to convert natural rubber into a more durable material thanks to the addition of sulphur.

Curing rubber has been carried out since prehistoric times by the Aztecs and others, but the process of vulcanisation was developed in the 19th century by Charles Goodyear in America and Thomas Hancock in Britain at almost the same time. It was named for Vulcan, the Roman god of fire (see above).

Charles Goodyear (1800-1860) was a self-taught chemist who ran a successful agricultural tools and hardware business but after a bout of ill-health he went bankrupt. He then spent five years hunting for a more stable form of rubber that wouldn't degrade with time. He worked on his experiments while imprisoned for debt.

He had some initial success, despite nearly gassing himself, but then his company making life preservers and rubber shoes was crushed by the financial crisis known as the Panic of 1837.

Bouncing back, he continued his work and stumbled upon the idea of using heat in his process.

The Goodyear Tire & Rubber company was not founded by Charles, but it was named in his honour forty years after his death.

Thomas Hancock (1786-1865) spent his early career as a coach builder. This inspired him to make waterproof fabrics to protect passengers on his coaches from the British weather. During the 1820s Hancock worked with Mackintosh (see the Style Icons chapter) to develop the double-textured fabric that would make a "mac" a household word. They merged their companies and progressed despite their factories burning down, twice.

His younger brother, Walter Hancock was also an inventor, chiefly of steam-powered road vehicles.

To Conclude

Those pesky Greeks donated loads of words to the English language, especially eponyms. It's trickier to become an ancient Greek god than to get your name in the dictionary but think of the side benefits. You get immortality, good looks (unless you're Vulcan), fun punishing impertinent mortals, battles with titans, a pretty cool temple for your worshippers and of course, Mount Olympus to live in.

Perhaps being a Greek god would be *better* than getting your name into the dictionary, but don't forget they belonged to a dysfunctional family and not many people believe in them anymore.

8
Your Country Needs YOU

Wars aren't a good thing, unless you sell arms. However they are rather good at spurring on inventions and bringing fame to unlikely heroes. Both activities provide opportunities to get your name into the dictionary. If you get called up to serve your country your chances of a dictionary spot improve, especially if you come back alive.

You will also find a selection of army items in the Style Icon chapter. The world of fashion loves trend-setters from the army, navy, and air force.

Berserk

{with thanks to Peter Sheehan at Peter Sheehan Studio}

To go berserk means to act in a crazy and particularly aggressive way.

This was suggested by a Wordfoolery reader who spends his spare time being an extra on the "Vikings" television series, so I assume he goes "berserk at work".

The word berserk entered English in the 19th century as a noun used to describe an ancient Norse warrior who fought with uncontrolled ferocity. They struck down anybody nearby, seemed to be unaffected by fire or iron, and bit their shields. The term berserker is also used.

Berserk, which we now use to describe frantic or angry activity, was a direct borrowing from the Norse word berserkr which is formed by combining two words – bjorn (bear) and serkr (coat).

The original berserkers were champion warriors, mainly in Icelandic tales, who fought in a trance-like state of anger. They were known for battling without armour. They wore animals skins instead. There were three main codes for this form of Northern martial art – bear, boar, and wolf and with the coming of Christianity these became emblems on knights' shields.

The berserker warriors may have been part of a bear cult. There are accounts in the sagas of them being laid on bear pelts for their funerals. The bear was one of the animals associated with Odin, the father of the Norse gods, so by wearing it they sought his strength and approval.

Bear warrior symbolism survives to this day in armies. The guards of the Danish and British monarchs, the Queen's Guard and the Royal Life Guards, both wear bearskin caps.

In 1015 Norway outlawed berserkers and the same happened in Iceland. By the 12th century berserker war-bands had disappeared.

The Lewis Chessmen, ancient Norse chess pieces found on the Isle of Lewis in the Outer Hebrides, Scotland, include berserkers biting their shields.

Bogey

A bogey was originally a Scottish goblin from the 1500s onwards but it has also come to mean "one over par" in golfing terms. Par itself pre-dates bogey. In stock-exchange terminology par was the normal price for a stock.

In 1890 Hugh Rotherham was the secretary of the golf club in Coventry (see the "Location, Location, Location" chapter). He proposed standardising the number of shots a good golfer should take to get around their course. He called that number the ground score. The secretary of Great Yarmouth Golf Club adopted the idea. At one match Major Charles Wellman exclaimed "One of your players is a regular bogeyman" and the ground score became the bogey score.

Players of the time thought they were playing against a real Mr. Bogey when they measured themselves against the bogey score. Bogey was interchangeable with the term par.

In 1892 the secretary of the United Services Club at Gosport, U.S.A. calculated bogey for their club but the servicemen didn't think they should play against a mere mister so Bogey was promoted to Colonel Bogey.

Bogey changed to its current one-over-par meaning in the early 20th century. As golf became more popular in America the standards of play rose and par was defined more accurately for courses, but many British courses didn't adjust their bogey scores to reflect this. Americans, especially professional players, began referring to one over par as bogey, much to British chagrin.

Furphy

In informal, mainly Australian, usage a furphy is an unfounded rumour.

Furphy was derived from the Furphy company who supplied water and sanitation carts in Australia, and elsewhere, during World War I. Their name was printed on the tanks and buckets used by the troops and they came to describe the war news and gossip circulated at the these spots. The furphy chat seems to pre-date the more modern "water-cooler gossip".

Given that furphies dealt with sanitation too, there is likely to be a connection to excretion as well. Perhaps the soldiers rated the official war news as being rather useless?

The cart drivers moved from camp to camp and hence were good sources of war news, although it wasn't always reliable. They parked their carts near the latrines, one of the few spots where the soldiers were out of sight and earshot of their commanding officers and hence free to gossip.

The furphy cart was invented by John Furphy (1842-1920) in the 1880s. He was an experienced wheel-wright and made the cylindrical water tanks on wheels to bring water to farms for agricultural and domestic use. The cast-iron tanks were pulled by horses. In 1945 the chassis was improved and rubber-tyres added to the wheels.

Over the years Furphy used the sides of the tank to inspire and advertise. He was a keen church-goer and included messages such as "produce and populate or perish" and "water is the gift of God, but beer is a concoction of the devil, come and have a drink of water". The furphy tanks, produced by the family firm, are still used today during Australia's dry season.

Geronimo

Geronimo is perhaps the most fun yodel to call when diving in recklessly.

Geronimo (1829-1909), whose name translates as "the one who yawns", was an Apache leader and warrior in the Bedonkohe band. His band joined with others to carry out raids and resistance to the U.S. and Mexican armies following the end of the Mexican-American war in 1848 as Americans began to settle the Apache lands.

Geronimo was not an Apache chief but many followed him due to his skill in raiding and revenge warfare for more than thirty years. He was particularly driven to avenge the murder of his first wife, mother, and children by Mexicans. He was not always a popular leader but he was respected and believed to have healing skills and the ability to foresee the future. Legends surrounded him over time. Tales of him slipping away from trouble through secret escape routes abound.

He was forced to surrender several times during his escapes from the reservations. He finally accepted life on an Apache reservation in Arizona as a prisoner of war in 1886. He became a Christian although there's evidence to suggest that conversion was skin-deep.

He became a celebrity in his old age, writing his autobiography in 1905 with presidential permission from Roosevelt and attending the St. Louis World Fair in 1904 where he signed autographs.

Geronimo had nine wives during his lifetime.

He died of complications following a fall from his horse at the age of 80. His final words were reported to be, "I should have never surrendered. I should have fought until I was the last man alive".

Thanks to a 1939 movie about Geronimo, U.S. paratroopers shout Geronimo as they leap from airplanes.

Guns

A huge number of guns are named for their inventors. Here's a brief selection.

Colt Revolver

Invented by Samuel Colt (1814-1862). Inspired by a science encyclopedia and overhearing soldiers talking about the impossibility of a gun that could discharge more than five times without reloading Samuel decided to create the impossible gun. His early inventions struggled and he was regularly in trouble at school for blowing things up, but his company took off when the Texas Rangers ordered a thousand guns for the American war with Mexico. In the American Civil War he supplied both sides. He was a pioneer in advertising, marketing, and early assembly line production methods. He became one of the wealthiest men in America.

Derringer

A single-shot small pocket pistol invented by Henry Deringer (1786-1868). Henry's early gun-smithing included making trade rifles for Native American tribes to fulfill U.S. treaty obligations. He never patented his pocket pistol and it was widely copied. John Wilkes Booth shot President Lincoln with a derringer.

Gatling Gun

A hand-cranked, rapid-fire early precursor to the machine gun invented by Richard Jordan Gatling (1818-1903). It was used by Union forces in the American Civil War. General Custer famously chose not to bring gatlings with him to the Battle of Little Big Horn, also known as Custer's Last Stand. Gatling dedicated his life to inventing. He created ways to improve toilets, bicycles, cleaning of wool, pneumatic power, a steam-driven tractor, a screw propeller, and of course, guns. He made and lost several fortunes during his lifetime.

Kalashnikov Rifle

An automatic rifle whose most popular model is the AK-47, invented by Mikhail Kalashnikov (1919-2013). He was a Russian general, inventor, and poet who insisted his ultra-reliable weapon was for defence, not offence. He claimed he would have preferred to have designed a lawn mower but he was a soldier and wanted to create a reliable gun for soldiers. Approximately a million of these rifles are produced annually, about half of them illegal copies. The Kalashnikov features on the flag of

Mozambique.

Luger Pistol

A semi-automatic pistol patented by Austrian Georg J. Luger (1849-1923) in 1898. Luger was a soldier in the Austro-Hungarian army and thanks to his good marksmanship became an instructor at their firearms school where he developed an interest in small-arms design. He created the luger after leaving the military. The luger was used by the Germans in both World Wars and by many fictional villains since then.

Tommy Gun

The Thompson submachine gun which became notorious during American prohibition era was invented in 1918 by John T. Thompson (1860-1940). It had many nicknames including "the Chicago typewriter" because of its association with gangsters and police alike. Thompson came from an army family and designed weapons in the Army Ordnance Department. He, unusually for the time, tested guns on donated human corpses and cattle to assess effectiveness. He retired from the army when America didn't initially join World War I and joined the Remington Arms company where he developed the early form of the tommy gun. When America entered the war he re-joined the army. After the war he re-joined civilian life and continued to develop his trench-sweeping gun. He died shortly before the advent of World War II caused the U.S. army to order his gun in large quantities.

Uzi Submachine Gun

The first version of this gun was designed by German-born Israeli gun designer Major Uziel Gal in the late 1940s. He fled Germany in 1933, settling first in the U.K. and later in the British Mandate of Palestine. He designed the gun shortly after the establishment of Israel. It was adopted by the Israeli Defence Forces in 1951 and named after him against his wishes. He later moved to America to seek medical treatment for his daughter and continued his firearms design work there.

Winchester Rifle

The repeating rifle known as "the Gun that won the West". The Winchester was produced by the Winchester Repeating Arms Company which was named for Oliver Winchester, the largest share-holder. The company grew from the earlier design work by Smith and Wesson. Horace Smith (1808-1893) started his gun-making career creating guns to shoot whales. Daniel B. Wesson (1825-1906) eloped to marry against his father-in-law's objection that he was a mere gunsmith who would amount to nothing. He was a strong advocate for homeopathy and founded a homeopathic hospital in 1900. It converted to mainstream medicine after his death.

Martinet

A martinet is a strict disciplinarian who expects to be obeyed in every last detail. The term dates to the reign of King Louis XIV (1638-1715) of France, the Sun King. His army was somewhat chaotic, but fortunately for Louis it contained Lieutenant Colonel Jean Martinet who, when made Inspector General of the infantry, created a rigorous system of drilling and discipline. He wasn't adverse to the use of the cat-o-nine-tails on errant soldiers either.

The weapon of infantry at the time was the musket and Martinet trained his troops to fire in precise group volleys to overcome the musket's terrible accuracy issues. It was a case of "if you all fire at once, you've got a chance of hitting something and frightening the enemy". He also got them advancing in neat lines, pushed out the mercenaries who'd formed the core of most armies, and introduced the bayonet. Martinet's name became associated with strict military discipline and gradually came to mean any strict disciplinarian in the wider world.

Martinet was killed in a friendly-fire incident at the siege of Duisberg in 1672, perhaps by one of those perfect volleys.

Sam Browne Belt

This is a high visibility belt worn by cyclists in low light conditions. It is also a wide leather belt with a diagonal strap over the shoulder to the waist common in military uniforms.

This belt was originally a belt for a sword or pistol and was designed by Samuel J. Browne (1824-1901). He was born in India and had a distinguished military career in the British army. He earned the Victoria Cross medal for his role in the Indian Mutiny (1857-1859) and became a general in 1888.

Originally an officer's sword hung on a small clasp, called a frog, from their jacket or trouser belt but the sword slid around during charges and had to be steadied before being drawn, wasting valuable seconds. In 1857, as a captain, Browne was charging a cannon position and received two wounds which left him without a left hand.

He found he was now unable to draw his sword. He improvised his new belt, along with clips for binoculars, and a pistol holster. Soon other officers copied his design. It eventually became standard issue.

In the period between World War I and II, the belt became a fashion for European and American women.

Shanghaied or Shanghai Press

Shanghaiing is the practice of kidnapping people to serve as crew on sailing ships. Pressing or press ganging is the related term for kidnapping them to serve in the British Royal Navy.

Shanghaiing wasn't that common in Shanghai, it was the destination port rather than the source in most of these tales. Sailors and bystanders would be shanghaied from London, Bristol, Hull, San Francisco, Portland, New York, Boston etc.

The practice arose due to a chronic lack of experienced sailors in the mid 1800s. This was due, in part, to crews absconding en masse to try their hand in the California Gold Rush.

Once a sailor signed on for a voyage it was against the law for him to leave before it was over. Boarding masters were in charge of sourcing enough sailors for the crew and they got paid per person so they had a big incentive to get someone on board, even if they had to get them drunk first or forge their signature on the crew list.

The shanghai press wasn't finally outlawed until 1915 when the end of the age of sail meant the demand for crew was less urgent.

In Chinese the word Shanghai means "upon the sea".

Shrapnel

Shrapnel is the term for fragments of a bomb thrown out upon explosion.

Henry Shrapnel (1761-1842) used his spare time to invent the shrapnel shell which is designed to explode and scatter debris. He originally called it the spherical case shell. He spent years developing it and demonstrated it at Gibraltar in 1787. His invention was finally adopted by the British army in 1803 and used against the Dutch in Surinam.

Shrapnel shells were vital during the Peninsular War and the ultimate defeat of Napoleon at Waterloo in 1815. They were used up to the end of World War I. Shrapnel shells were used at the Battle of the Somme in a vain attempt to cut the barbed wire in no-man's-land. Sadly this misunderstanding of their effective use probably led to the high casualty count in the battle.

Shrapnel was promoted for his efforts but given scant financial recompense.

There is a super-villain in the DC comic book universe called Shrapnel. He's made of organic metal and can fire off bits of himself as explosions.

Stonewall

To stonewall is to resist in a defensive manner, perhaps by refusing to communicate.

This technique is named for Thomas Jonathan Jackson (1824-1863), a Confederate general in the American Civil War. His nickname was Stonewall Jackson thanks to his troops standing their ground like a stone wall in the face of attack and hence turning the tide of the first Battle of Bull Run.

Stonewall was the best known Confederate commander after General Robert E. Lee. Some of his battle strategies are still studied to this day. His troops became renowned for moving position rapidly and it earned them the nickname of "foot cavalry".

His early life was tough, losing both parents at a young age and the war lost him a sister too as she supported the other side. His sister Laura was a staunch Unionist, to the point where although she later mourned his death she was glad he wasn't helping the Confederate army anymore.

He believed in and actively helped the education of African American slaves.

His own pickets accidentally shot him at the Battle of Chancellorsville in 1863. He lost an arm as a result and died of pneumonia eight days later.

During a training exercise in 1921 a U.S. marine commander was informed by a local farmer than Jackson's arm was buried nearby under a marker. He dismissed the idea and to prove the farmer wrong dug at the spot, unearthing a wooden box with an arm in it. He re-buried it and placed a plaque on the marker.

Tommy

A tommy is slang for an enlisted British soldier.

The full name is actually Tommy Atkins and it was in use from the 1800s but it became established in World War I.

Legend has it that the Duke of Wellington chose the name as a generic soldier's name when he was impressed by a common soldier's bravery at the Battle of Boxtel in 1794. After a fierce encounter he spotted a Private Thomas Atkins and complimented him on a good job. The man replied "It's all in a day's work, sir" and died shortly thereafter.

In 1815 the War Office chose Tommy Atkins as a sample name in the army infantry account book – basically giving an example of how a soldier should sign his name or make his mark to claim his pay. This use continued up to World War I.

It may also have been the sample name on enlisting sheets used in World War I with underage combatants giving it as a false name to disguise their age.

Yankee

Yankee as a term has two related, but different meanings on either side of the Atlantic Ocean. In British English, a Yankee is anybody from the United States of America whereas in American usage it refers to someone from the northern states, particularly New England. Yankee has also entered several other languages to mean an American, but with many spelling variations.

The word Yankee may have originally come from the name Jan Kass (meaning John Cheese), a nickname for Dutch settlers in the New World. When the Dutch settled New York they applied the name to their neighbours in north Connecticut.

By the time of the War of Independence the British used it for any colonist. The song "Yankee Doodle" originally mocked the poorly clad soldiers of the colonial army, but those troops took the song, changed the lyrics and made it into a marching tune. Today it is Connecticut's state song.

During the American Civil War Yankee was used by southern troops to derisively describe soldiers on the Union side. By World War I allied troops described any American solider as a Yankee or just yank and the name entered popular use.

One tongue-in-cheek joke has it that "a Yankee is someone from the North that visits the South. A damn Yankee is one who moves here."

In Cockney rhyming slang a yank is a septic tank.

Conclusion

Wars and warriors have contributed many words to the English language and surprisingly many of them are unrelated to battle. From golf-scores to gossip, the soldiers and sailors of past conflicts have played their part in the dictionary.

9
Be a Political Animal

If joining the army appears too dangerous an occupation to get your name in the dictionary then here's a less high-risk career – politics. However it is only fair to point out that even this arena carries dangers such as assassination, coup d'etat, revolutions, and the most perilous of all – elections.

What politics lacks in job security it makes up for with the power to effect change and enough fame to propel you, perhaps, into the pages of that elusive dictionary. As some of these entries prove, success in politics isn't essential to inclusion and even those who ended their political careers on the wrong end of a dagger have contributed to the English language.

You may wonder at the exclusion of Wellington and Gladstone from this political section given that they were British Prime Ministers. You will find Wellington in the "Be Irish" chapter and Gladstone, and his bag, is happy in the "If you want to get ahead, Get a Hat" chapter.

Borked

Bork is an American slang verb meaning to defeat the candidacy of a person for public office through a campaign of harsh criticism. The term comes from conservative judge Robert Heron Bork (1927-2012) who in 1987 was subjected to such an attack when he was nominated by Ronald Reagan for the U.S. Supreme Court. The verb is also used to describe a broken object. For example, "Since I installed that last upgrade my laptop is totally borked."

Bork had a distinguished career in the law and crossed paths with occupants of the Oval Office several times. In 1973 President Nixon wanted to fire Archibald Cox (the Watergate special prosecutor) for seeking tapes of Oval Office conversations. His Attorney General refused, as did the deputy attorney general. This left Bork as acting AG and he did the firing, an act that was later found to have been illegal. In the years after Watergate, when Bork was a professor at Yale Law School, his students included Bill and Hillary Clinton.

Following his defeat at the hands of the U.S. Senate he resigned as a judge and amongst other jobs worked as legal counsel to Mitt Romney's presidential campaign in 2011.

For those of us in the European part of the world bork is inextricably linked with the Swedish Chef on "The Muppets" whose classic line was "bork, bork, bork" long before Robert Bork's failed candidacy.

Caesarean Section

Caesarean section, also known as c-section, is the use of surgery to deliver one or more babies. In many cases such an operation is life-saving for the mother and child. The technique dates back to 715 B.C. when it would be used after the death of the mother in an attempt to save the child. Mothers surviving didn't occur until the 1500s. With the advent of antiseptics and anaesthetics in the 1800s the survival rate improved dramatically. About 23 million c-sections are carried out globally each year.

Ancient tales of c-sections abound worldwide with stories from India, China, Irish mythology, Iranian legends, and the Babylonian Talmud but the one that snagged the name was Pliny the Elder's recounting of Julius Caesar's ancestor being born by c-section. Pliny noted that the family name dated from this feat as it comes from caedere, the Latin verb "to cut".

Yes, his ancestor, not Julius Caesar (100-44 B.C.).

Additionally, Julius' own mother survived childbirth, thus ruling out his delivery by c-section as mother mortality was 100% at that point in Roman history. So although the procedure is named after him, he was not born in this manner.

Amazingly there have been some rare cases of mothers having to perform a c-section on themselves. Inés Ramírez Pérez of Mexico carried out a successful c-section on herself in 2000.

As noted in the Tickle Tastebuds chapter, Julius Caesar had nothing to do with Caesar salad either.

His first name is commemorated in the month of July. He renamed the seventh month from Quintilis to July in his own honour in 46 B.C. during his reform of the Roman calendar.

His surname did enter English in one way, but really it belongs to his wife. Julius Caesar divorced his second wife, Pompeia, in 62 B.C. as she was linked in rumour to Publius Clodius, a notorious dissolute of the time who had interrupted a sacred female rite disguised as a woman with the intent of seducing Pompeia.

The phrase "Caesar's wife must be above reproach", or the shortened form "Caesar's wife" refers to someone who is honest and totally moral. It was Julius' response, at trial, as to why he divorced her if she were innocent.

Caesar, despite renaming July, and a great many military and political victories came to a grim end on the Ides of March (15th of March) 44 B.C. when he was assassinated by a group of senators led by Marcus Junius Brutus. His adopted son became the first Roman Emperor.

Chauvinism

{thanks to Dianne Thomas at www.diannethomas.net }

Despite links to "male chauvinism" this word actually means excessive, unthinking devotion to one's country.

Nicolas Chauvin of Rochefort (born 1780), a soldier in the First Army of the French Republic and later in Napoleon's Grand Army, was wounded 17 times and he was ridiculed for his unswerving devotion to his leader and country even when he was released from that army with a meagre pension, a medal, and a ceremonial sabre.

Charles and Jean Cogniard made Chauvin famous in their comedy "Le Cocarde Tricolore" in 1831 which featured him as a young and over-enthused recruit. Support for Napoleon by that time was not popular. Chauvin later featured in other French comedies and the word spread into English.

Research has failed to turn up many facts about

Chauvin's existence, leading some historians to speculate that he was an entirely fictional creation. However the devotion of Napoleon's troops, especially those that served with him on early campaigns, was legendary so his existence is likely.

In more recent times chauvinism has come to mean fanatical devotion and unreasoned belief in the superiority of your group and cause over all others, as in the case of male chauvinism. Male chauvinism's first documented use as a term was in the 1935 play "Till the Day I Die" by Clifford Odets.

The English term jingoism has retained the original meaning of chauvinism more clearly.

Gerrymander

To redraw election boundaries, or any rules, in your own favour. The process creates outlandishly-shaped electoral districts.

American politician Elbridge Gerry (1744-1814), while Governor of Massachusetts in 1810, sought to do this.

The story goes that one day the painter Gilbert Stuart visited the offices of "The Boston Sentinel". He saw the new district map and added head, wings, and claws to it.

"That will do for a salamander", he said.

"A Gerrymander you mean," replied Benjamin Russell, the editor.

Elkanah Tisdale drew a political cartoon of the idea, possibly for the Boston Gazette, and carved woodblocks to enable its printing. The woodblocks are preserved in the Library of Congress.

Gerry's party won the election as the result of his meddling, but he lost his own job. Gerry went on to become Vice President 1813-1814. He died just 18 months into his vice-presidency and he is the only signatory of the Declaration of Independence to be buried in Washington D.C.

The concept of "redistricting" pre-dates Elbridge Gerry. In 1788 the former governor of Virginia persuaded the state legislature to reshape the 5th district to force his political enemy James Madison to run against James Monroe, assuming in such a contest that Madison would lose. To his surprise Madison won and went on to become the 4th U.S. President. The 5th President was Monroe.

Guess who was Madison's vice president? Elbridge Gerry. Perhaps he taught his gerrymandering technique to the highest office in the land. His district modification skills may have been questionable but Gerry was an important statesman in the history of America. He helped draft the Bill of Rights. He had enduring friendships in all parties and opposed the idea of parties entirely.

Gerrymander is a portmanteau word, blending two words together, as well as an eponym.

Luddite

A luddite is a person who is opposed to industrial innovation and new technology.

Ned Ludd was a young 18th century labourer who, in 1779, destroyed two labour-saving stocking frames at his workplace. His name became associated with anyone who destroys machines and with time evolved into a fictional King Ludd who like Robin Hood was alleged to live in Sherwood Forest.

In 1811-1816 a group of English textile workers and self-employed weavers, worried that technology would render skilled workers obsolete, formed a movement to protest about these new machines. They tried to destroy the new textile machines in the midlands and north of England.

At one time there were more members of the British army fighting the luddites than there were fighting Napoleon on the Iberian Peninsula. When some luddites attacked mill owners and killed one a group of 60 of them were rounded up and sent to court for a show trial. Although 30 were acquitted, the rest were sentenced to hanging or transportation, thus effectively ending the movement.

In the 1830s there was similar push by agricultural workers to break threshing machines during the Swing riots.

Marxism

Marxism is a theory of socialism proposed by Karl Marx (1818-1883) and Friedrich Engels (1820-1895).

Marx was born in Prussia to a middle class family and a lawyer father. He was educated in the universities of Bonn and Berlin. As a student he joined a group called the Young Helegians who criticised the political and cultural establishments of the day.

He became a journalist and later an editor of a radical newssheet. When authorities suppressed his newspaper he moved to Paris where he met Engels. Later in Brussels he wrote "The Communist Manifesto" (1848).

He was expelled by Germany, France, and Belgium.

In 1849 he settled in London where he lived for the rest of his life despite being denied British citizenship. He further developed his theories about the economies of capitalism and class struggle in "Das Kapital" whose first volume was published in 1867. He worked on subsequent volumes for the rest of his life but never finished them.

Despite being one of the most famous economists ever he was always short of cash himself. Engels supported him.

Marx once fought a duel with another student.

He was the son of Jewish parents who converted to being Lutheran in 1816 to circumvent anti-semitc laws. Marx was Lutheran too, initially, but became atheist later.

Marx married an educated Baroness from the Prussian ruling elite who'd known him since childhood. Despite her controversially breaking a suitable engagement for the marriage, he befriended her father. He wrote several unpublished love poems to her.

Lenin built the Russian Revolution (1917) on Marx's ideals, so Marx became famous long after his death.

Ironically it was Tsar Nicholas I of Russia who had requested that Marx's first newspaper be suppressed by the Prussian government.

Marx is buried in London's Highgate Cemetery which is a famous Victorian graveyard, nature reserve, and historic park.

Being a Political Animal

Being a political animal isn't easy. Chauvin was mocked for devotion, Marx had little success in his lifetime, and Bork had his reputation ruined with very little cause.

However, people notice politicians. They may not agree with them but they talk about them, and their schemes. Sometimes, that's all it takes to get your name into the English language.

10
Are You a Style Icon?

Dedicated followers of fashion love a new trend but the ones to watch for dictionary inclusion are the fashion-forward types who set the trend. They may be a soldier wearing an item for pure practicality. You won't find too many elegant ladies sashaying around this chapter but you will find items of clothing with an eponymous name and an intriguing back story.

Many eponymous fabrics have fascinating histories too, often linked to the town of their original manufacture – making them toponyms. These are included at the end of this chapter.

Strictly speaking the Duke of Wellington should be in this chapter but I couldn't resist placing him in the Irish chapter. Likewise you will find Balaclava and other head-gear in the Hat chapter.

Blazer

In the early days of the Royal Navy captains were allowed to issue whatever clothes they deemed fit to their crew out of their own pockets. As a result most crews didn't wear a uniform but some of the richer captains issued uniforms for ceremonial events.

The crew of the HMS Harlequin wore harlequin outfits. The crew of the HMS Caledonia wore tartan. The unfortunate crew of the HMS Tulip had to wear green suits with flowers in their caps. The HMS Blazer adopted a navy jacket teamed with blue and white striped jerseys. Over time the navy blue look became standard within the navy.

Bloomers

Bloomers are a loose, gathered-at-the-knee undergarment for women.

American publisher, women's rights activist and journalist Amelia Jenks Bloomer (1818-1894) introduced a style of dress to the world, but it wasn't the bloomers which bear her name.

She wore an entire outfit designed by Elizabeth Smith Miller (who introduced Bloomer to this form of dress) to a ball in Lowell, Massachusetts in 1851. It consisted of a loose-fitting tunic, a short knee-length skirt, and billowing Turkish style trousers gathered at the ankle. It sounds like a female version of the genie from "Aladdin" but perhaps a little more covered up.

Her style created controversy because trousers were seen as clothes for only the male of the species. She was campaigning for less restrictive clothing for women in an era where women wore corsets so severe that they displaced internal organs, and many layers of petticoats some weighted down at the hem.

The circulation of her journal soared as a result of the campaign. After her style statement she was swamped with letters from women around the country looking for a pattern for the outfit. Women who lectured on the cause of women's right to vote began to wear the outfits too, although after a few years they returned to more traditional dress as they felt it was distracting from their arguments.

Some of the nurses in the American Civil War wore the costume as it was practical for their work.

Later bloomers came to describe the trousers of the outfit, then the knee-length knickerbockers (see below) worn by cyclists – especially during the 1890s cycling craze. Now bloomers are just strangely voluminous undergarments.

Amelia became a teacher after leaving school and then a governess. While working as a governess she met Dexter Bloomer. After marriage she wrote about social issues for the newspaper he edited. In 1848 she founded "The Lily" a temperance newspaper that also promoted women's rights.

She and her husband continued writing and publishing. She became involved in the women's suffrage movement. She is credited with helping to get women the right to vote in Ohio in 1873.

The Amelia Bloomer Project honours the top feminist books for young readers each year.

Bloomer may have begun the movement to normalise women wearing trousers in 1851 but it took significant time to complete the job. In 1919 a Puerto Rican woman was jailed for the crime of wearing trousers. By the late 1920s and 1930s it had become acceptable. Then during World War II, with fabric in short supply, many women wore their husband's trousers, cut to size, while they were away fighting, particularly as trousers were practical work wear.

In 1969 Charlotte Reid became the first woman to wear trousers in the U.S. Congress. In 1989 Rebecca Morgan became the first in the U.S. Senate. Pat Nixon was the first First Lady to wear them in public.

Cardigan

A cardigan is a knitted jacket and was originally military attire. It started life as a knitted waistcoat worn by British officers in the Crimean War and they were named for their commander, Major General James Brudenell, the 7th Earl of Cardigan.

The earl rose to fame by leading the infamous, and disastrous, Charge of the Light Brigade at the Battle of Balaclava in 1854. The cardigan rose with him.

The action was immortalised by Alfred Lord Tennyson in his poem "The Charge of the Light Brigade".

The 7th earl survived the charge and told the tale to Queen Victoria and the rest of an adoring London, but a sixth of his men did not. Afterwards many doubts arose as to the competence of those in command but the public had already bought cardigans galore in honour of their hero and the garment has rarely been out of fashion since.

The Crimean War (1853-1856) was clearly a cold affair and many of the official warm uniform supplies for British troops didn't arrive in time, hence the rise of the knitted cardigans and balaclavas, although the first use of the term for the head warmer didn't happen until 30 years after the battle. So when you throw on a cardigan spare a thought for the poor, frozen soldiers of the Crimean War.

Garibaldi

A garibaldi can be one of three things. It's a loose woman's blouse with long sleeves. It's a biscuit with a layer of currants. It's Giuseppe Garibaldi (1807-1882) the Italian patriot and soldier who united the Italian states into one nation.

There's a story behind him giving his name to the woman's blouse and it doesn't involve him cross-dressing. He and his men, the thousand risorgimento, in the Italian nationalist movement wore red shirts presented to them by the government of Uruguay.

Garibaldi was born in Nice, a city which today is firmly in France but back then rulers passed it around like a slice of cake. He followed the family business by going to sea and becoming a ship's captain. While travelling he met some Italians seeking to free their country from Austrian rule and decided to join them. He took part in a failed uprising in Piedmont, was sentenced to death in his absence, and had to flee the country. He ended up in Brazil.

He again got involved in resistance work there. He met and married one of the Brazilian fighters, Anita. They settled in Uruguay where he became a trader and teacher and he adopted the red shirt, poncho, and sombrero of the gauchos. He raised an Italian Legion to fight in the Uruguayan Civil War and they copied his style. He gained considerable battle and guerilla warfare experience but the fate of his homeland was always on his mind.

He returned to Italy with Anita during the civil unrest of 1848 with a core band of his soldiers at his back. They eventually had to retreat from defeat in Rome and Anita, who was carrying their fifth child, died during the retreat. He was forced to flee again, this time to work as a sea captain from Staten Island in New York.

He returned to Italy in 1854, and settled to a quiet farming life but the country was still seeking independence from France and Austria, and Garibaldi couldn't resist the call. In 1860 he raised his one thousand men and they donned their red shirts. They conquered Sicily, Naples, and left the Piedmont crown to unite the south of Italy with the north, all while wearing those shirts.

Garibaldi offered his services to Lincoln in the American

Civil War but would only take part if the aim of the war was declared to be the abolition of slavery, a position Lincoln could not take at that point.

In 1879 at the age of 72 he founded the League of Democracy to campaign for votes for all men and women, the maintenance of a standing Italian army, and the abolition of church property.

He died, aged 82, having fought in nearly every major war of his age in Europe.

Garibaldi biscuits are named after him, but there's no story of him eating them.

Each year within the Six Nations Rugby Championship the winner of the France versus Italy game is awarded the Garibaldi Trophy.

Knickerbockers

Knickerbockers are short baggy trousers gathered at the knee.

Dietrich Knickerbocker was the pseudonym of the author Washington Irving (1783-1859) when he wrote the satirical "History of New York from the Beginning of the World to the End of the Dutch Dynasty" in 1809. The book's title was shortened to "Knickerbocker's History of New York" and knickerbocker came to mean an honest Dutch citizen descended from the original settlers of New York.

Then when George Cruikshank (1792-1878) illustrated the British edition of the book he depicted the Dutch settlers in baggy trousers gathered at the knee and they acquired the name too.

There was an actual Mr. Knickerbocker. Herman Knickerbocker (1779-1855) was a friend of Irving. Herman was descended from Harmen Jansen van Wijhe who added Knickerbocker to the end of his name upon landing in the New World in 1682 so ultimately the name was entirely an invention.

The first ever organised baseball team was the Knickerbockers of Manhattan.

The word is also the full name of the New York Knicks basketball team which was founded in 1946 and their logo features Father Knickerbocker, complete with the eponymous short trousers.

Plus fours and plus twos worn by golfers are a variant of knickerbockers. Plus fours extend four inches below the knee, plus twos extend two inches below the knee.

Knickerbockers were popular in early bicycling circles and are still part of the uniform for fencing. They are sometimes called knickers but beware as that's also the term for ladies' underwear in British English.

The famous tall ice-cream sundae with a mixture of ice-cream, fruit, cream, and a cherry on top is called a knickerbocker glory and is particularly popular in the British Isles. It dates to the 1920s, the knickerbocker trousers' zenith. The origin of its name is uncertain but may be linked to the Knickerbocker hotel in New York although it only operated from 1906 to 1921 on Times Square before Prohibition put it, and its lavish parties, out of business.

Leotard

A leotard is a close-fitting one piece, skin-tight garment worn by ballet dancers, acrobats, and gymnasts.

The leotard was designed by Jules Léotard (1838-1870) for his work in the circus and he called it a maillot which was a general French word for tight-fitting clothes.

Jules was a famous acrobat in London and Paris but he was a qualified lawyer too. He learned his early routines over a swimming pool. He perfected the first aerial somersault and invented the flying trapeze.

Léotard inspired the 1860 song "That Daring Young Man on the Flying Trapeze" by George Leybourne.

The word leotard was only used in 1886, many years after his death of smallpox at age 32.

Levis

Levis are the trademark name for a type of jeans designed by Levi Strauss (1830-1902).

Strauss was a Bavarian immigrant and San Francisco clothing merchant at the time of the Gold Rush. He headed west to join the rush, but made his fortune running a dry goods store instead. He made tents and durable jeans in the 1850s, adding rivets in the 1870s to the corners of pockets so you could load the pockets with ore samples. He patented the process and the official blue jean was born.

Levi was involved in other businesses too and gave generously to various charities. He funded 28 scholarships at University of California Berkeley in 1897 which still run today.

In World War II jeans were declared an essential

commodity and were sold only to those engaged in war work.

Albert Einstein wore Levis.

Mackintosh

It rains a bit in Scotland so it is unsurprising that Scottish men invented the classic raincoat, or mac, a raincoat made of rubberised cloth.

The mac is named after the Scottish chemist Charles Macintosh (1760-1843) but it was another Scot, James Syme (1799-1870), who invented the basic process in 1823. Macintosh added the idea of sandwiching the fabrics together and focused on waterproofing. A few months later the fabric was patented by Macintosh and he founded a company in Glasgow making macs in 1830. The actual process is a method of sticking two layers of fabric together with rubber dissolved in naphtha.

In the 1830s Macintosh's company merged with Hancock's and they focused on rubberised coats to supply the British army, railway workers, and the police force.

Nightingale

A nightingale is a flannel scarf with sleeves, worn by patients sitting up in bed.

This garment has fallen from fashion but at one time was made by numerous Red Cross groups for the injured from World War I. They could be knitted but were usually made from flannel, a heavy brushed cotton.

The nightingale was named for Florence Nightingale (1820-1910) who is known for her work in the Crimean War. She worked in the military hospital in Scutari in 1854. She and her nurses sought to improve the conditions for the patients. The patients responded to her attentive care by dubbing her the Lady with the Lamp. The work of her team reduced the death rate there by two thirds.

After the Crimean War ended she devoted herself to improving the very low status of the nursing profession. She established St. Thomas' Hospital and training school for nurses. It was the first secular training college for nurses in the world and it is now part of King's College, London. Her writings sparked health care reform around the world. In 1883 she was awarded the Royal Red Cross by Queen Victoria. In 1907 she became the first woman to be awarded the Order of Merit from King Edward.

Florence Nightingale was born in Florence, Italy to a British family. She had a good education and became active in ministering to the tenants on her family's estate from a very young age. Her parents were outraged when she told them she wanted to be nurse as it was seen as a menial job. She turned down a marriage proposal and enrolled as a student nurse in Germany, despite their objections. Her father later gave her an allowance that allowed her to continue her work in nursing.

In the early 1850s she took a job in an English hospital and rose swiftly to be superintendent. She battled a cholera outbreak there. When the Crimea War began and English public opinion was worried about the treatment of injured soldiers, she received an invitation from the Secretary of War, a lifelong close friend, to take a corps of 34 nurses, mostly from religious orders, to fix matters.

The Crimean War took place before the experiments of Pasteur and Lister confirmed the existence, and danger, of germs. Once these were confirmed Florence included techniques for reducing infections and killing germs in her writings.

She contracted "Crimean fever", probably a form of extreme brucellosis, during her thirties thanks to her war work. She continued her work from her sick bed for the rest of her life. She consulted on managing field hospitals during the American Civil War.

The Nightingale Pledge is a variation of the Hippocratic oath taken by new nurses when they complete training. The Nightingale Medal is the highest international distinction a nurse can achieve.

Although her work opened the field of nursing to all women she referred to herself as a "man of action" and felt that women hadn't changed their lives as a result of her opinions whereas men had helped her to achieve much change.

She is buried in England but a monument to her was created by Francis William Sargent in 1913 and placed in the famous church of Santa Croce in Florence, Italy along with Michelangelo, Galileo, Rossini, and Machiavelli.

Petersham

Petersham is a tough corded ribbon used to stiffen belts and for hat bands. Petersham is sometimes confused with grosgrain ribbon. Grosgrain has a sealed edge and Petersham has a scalloped edge that is woven in with the rest of the ribbon. Petersham is woven so that when steamed it will take on a curved shape to match a fabric, for example in millinery.

Petersham was designed by an English army officer

called Charles Stanhope Viscount Petersham, the 4th Earl of Harrington (1780-1851). He was a well-known dandy and Regency Buck. He also designed, and popularised, a heavy woolen overcoat. The coat, and the ribbon which is still used today, came to be known by his name.

Petersham also invented an original mixture of snuff.

He was a Gentleman of the Bedchamber to Kings George III and IV. His family home in London was Harrrington House, now the Russian Embassy.

He never appeared in public before six p.m. and was known as Beau Petersham. His clothes, tea-drinking, and addiction to snuff were copied by the then Prince Regent. He owned 365 snuffboxes and used a different one each day. He designed many of his own clothes, which were then copied by an avid public. He created the Harrington hat too.

He married in his early 50s to a Covent Garden actress called Maria Foote who was 17 years his junior, much to his father's disapproval. Their only son died young so the title passed to his brother when he died.

Prince Albert

This style icon can be of two rather different types.

The first is a particular style of frockcoat popularised by Prince Albert of Saxe-Coburg and Gotha (1819-1861) who later became the Prince Consort of Queen Victoria.

The frockcoat given Albert's name was a dark double-breasted coat with a knee length skirt. The body of the coat tapers from shoulders to waist and it has long sleeves. Shoulder padding was not included. It was standard business attire during the Victorian era in Britain, and elsewhere.

The second Prince Albert is a penis piercing which is also named for Prince Albert. He allegedly wore a so-called "dressing ring" attached to his penis (possibly not via piercing) which was then strapped to his thigh in order to create a smooth line in the tight trousers of the day. This was a fairly common practice at the time. Needless to say, there's no proof Prince Albert actually did any of this, but the name has stuck.

Albert and Victoria were first cousins and nearly the same age. They were even assisted into the world by the same midwife. They survived two assassination attempts on them as a couple.

Victoria became queen at the age of 18. She proposed to him two years later. Albert died of typhoid when he was 42 and Victoria wore black and mourned him for the next forty years.

Popular legend has it that Prince Albert introduced the German custom of Christmas trees to Britain. This is unlikely to be true but the use of a tree by the Royal family no doubt popularised the concept.

Raglan Sleeve

A raglan sleeve is inset at a diagonal ang e from underarm to collar with no seam across the top of the shoulder. This gives more freedom of movement and a less structured look.

British Field Marshal Fitzroy James Henry Somerset, 1st Baron Raglan (1788-1855) served in the Napoleonic Wars and was wounded at Waterloo. The injury resulted in the amputation of his right arm. He is alleged to have bravely called back the medical staff afterwards, asking them to bring back his arm, because the ring his wife gave him was still on its finger.

He taught himself to write with his left hand, served as member of parliament, and became secretary to the

Duke of Wellington, who was Commander in Chief of the British Army. It was during the Crimean War that he became known for wearing a raglan sleeve and a loose fitting coat that went by the same name. His tailor had created the garments for him to help him with his disability.

He fought in the Crimean War despite the toll it took on his health. His tactics at the Battle of Balaclava were heavily criticised in the British press and he took some of the blame for the ill-fated Charge of the Light Brigade. He died in the Crimea from a combination of dysentery and depression.

Sideburns

Sideburns are strips of hair grown from a man's ears along the jawline.

Sideburns are named for Ambrose Everett Burnside (1824-1881). He was a general fighting for the Union side in the American Civil War. He was renowned not only for successful campaigns in North Carolina and Tennessee but also for the defeats he suffered at Fredericksburg and Petersburg.

After the war he was elected governor of Rhode Island,

and later senator. He was noted for his shaving habits. He sported side whiskers that joined his moustache, but paired with a clean-shaven chin. Over time his name was inverted to give us a term for them – sideburns.

Burnside was the first president of the N.R.A. (National Rifle Association) of America. He ran as a democrat before the Civil War but became a republican after the war.

Sideburns pre-dated Ambrose significantly. Alexander the Great is depicted wearing them in a mosaic found in the volcano-engulfed Roman city of Pompeii.

Tuxedo

{with thanks to Rick Ellrod at https://rickellrod.com/}

A tuxedo, tux, or dinner jacket is a formal evening suit, typically black, with a satin or grosgrain ribbon down the outer seam of the trouser leg. It is worn with a formal shirt and tie, or bowtie, and is what is called for when "black tie attire" is requested.

Dinner jackets appeared in England around 1887 as the emphasis on wearing a full tailcoat each evening for dinner gradually faded, possibly thanks to the wearing of a smoking jacket and tailored trousers by the Prince of

Wales at less formal dinners.

The tuxedo appeared a year later in the U.S. and was named for Tuxedo Park, a Hudson Valley enclave of New York's social elite where it was much worn in its early days. Thanks to a passing similarity to a Victorian smoking jacket the tuxedo is known as "smoking" in many European languages.

A tux is sometimes nicknamed a penguin or monkey suit.

Tuxedos weren't always black – grey and midnight blue were also popular choices.

Etiquette rules state that a boy shouldn't wear a dinner jacket before 15 or a tailcoat before they are 18.

Eponymous and Toponymous Fabrics

A surprising number of fabrics are named for people and places. Here's a short selection of their histories.

Bombast

Bombase is a heavy cotton used for menswear and padding – hence the use of bombast to mean extraneous words.

Bombast is with us since 1560s via Old French, late Latin, and the Greek word bombyx which meant silk but also sometimes referred to cotton. Bombast wriggled its way into the dictionary as bombastic, an adjective to describe pompous bluster.

Broderie Anglaise

Broderie anglaise is a delicate white cotton pierced with patterns edged with white thread. Literally translated this means English embroidery. It became associated with England thanks to its popularity there in the 19th century.

Calico

Calico is a plain woven cotton textile often made from unbleached and less processed cotton. It was dyed and printed in bright hues in Europe and became popular. The fabric originated in the city of Kozhikode in India which was known as Calicut to English traders.

Cherryderry

Cherryderry is a light cotton and silk blend with stripes or checks. It was used for women's dresses and handkerchiefs from the 17th century and was probably named for the Indian town of its manufacture.

Chino

Chino is a cotton twill fabric popular in trousers, often given the same name.

Chino and the chino trousers made from it are either named thanks to their toasted colour which is named chino in Spanish, or thanks to the original Chinese manufacturers of the cloth.

Crêpe de Chine or Crape

Crape is a thin silk or synthetic fabric with a crisp appearance, historically associated with Victorian mourning traditions.

This term entered English c. 1869 and translates as crepe from China, which of course is a major silk manufacturing nation. Oriental processes for its production were so secretive and valuable that different stages of the process were carried out in different towns far away from each other.

Damask

Damask is around from the early Middle Ages and was named for the city of Damascus on the Silk Road. It is a woven reversible fabric with the pattern woven into it.

Denim

Denim is a sturdy cotton warp-faced textile, the most common form being indigo denim where the warp thread is dyed blue but the weft is left white.

The name comes from "serge de Nîmes". The town of Nîmes in France was known for producing this twill style serge fabric.

Jeans themselves were named for the French term for Genoa in Italy where the first denim trousers were made.

Fustian

Fustian is a thick cotton cloth. Its name comes to English from medieval Latin "fustaneum" which relates to the town Fostat, near Cairo, where this cloth was made.

Holland

Holland is a fine linen sometimes striped with a coloured cotton warp. It is typically used for women's dresses and men's shirts and unsurprisingly was made in Holland.

Jersey

Jersey is a knit fabric used mostly for clothes such as t-shirts and draped dresses.

It was originally made from wool and originated in the island of Jersey in the Channel Islands which were known as exporters of knitted goods and textiles since medieval times. In 1916 Coco Chanel upset the fashion world by using jersey, then associated only with underwear, in outerwear garments.

Kersey

Kersey is a coarse woolen cloth which was important to the textile trade in medieval England. It takes its name from the village of Kersey in Suffolk, England although it was made in other places too.

Moleskin

Moleskin is a heavy cotton fabric with a brushed nap on one side which reminded wearers of a mole's skin. This was the work-wear fabric of choice in Europe from medieval times until the rise of jeans-wear in the 20th century as it is warm, durable, and wind resistant.

Paisley

Paisley is a distinctive curved pattern on fabric. The pattern is based on a pine-cone design from India and also has roots in Persia (Iran) in the 1800s.

Paisley's heyday in Europe came when the women of Paisley in Scotland used jacquard looms to weave "must have" woolen shawls with the pattern in the first half of the 19th century.

Tulle

Tulle is a knitted hexagonal net or mesh fabric. It's named for the city of Tulle in France where it was originally made in the 1700s. Queen Victoria popularised tulle by using it for her wedding dress but it is now best known for its use in ballet tutus.

Tweed

Tweed is a woven wool fabric. It was originally named tweel (the Scots for twill) but it was incorrectly transcribed in 1826 by a London clerk on an order-form and became tweed. The fabric was made in the valley of the River Tweed in Scotland (and elsewhere in Scotland and Ireland) so that helped the name to stick.

Style Icon Conclusions

Being a Style Icon is, perhaps, simpler in the social media age with vloggers and celebrities known worldwide. If you count yourself among them you may well find yourself edging into the dictionary, but as this chapter showed, there's no predicting what article of clothing or fabric will become popular next. Fashion is a fickle mistress.

11
Get your Name into a Popular Phrase

Dictionaries don't just list single words, they also list phrases and this might be the backdoor to the English language that you're seeking. It has worked for many before you, although sometimes their own stories were eclipsed by the phrase itself.

Darby and Joan

Darby and Joan is a phrase meaning a happily married older couple. It comes from these song lyrics -

"One summer afternoon we drove to my aunt and uncle's home for tea.

They were a real old Darby and Joan,

As much in love at 80 as they were at 18."

The song was written by Henry Woodfall (1686-1747), a printer who published many works by Alexander Pope. The song was published in "The Gentleman's Magazine" in 1735.

The original Darby and Joan are thought to have been John Darby, a printer in London who died in 1730, and his wife Joan. Woodfall served Darby as an apprentice. The couple died in their eighties and the Woodfall song may have been written in their honour, it is certainly the first known use of the phrase.

Since the 1940s many senior citizen clubs in Britain have opened and they are called Darby and Joan clubs, although they are open to all pensioners, regardless of name.

Fudging (the Books)

This expression and the general usage of fudging to mean obfuscating comes from Captain Fudge of *The Black Eagle*.

Lying Fudge, as he was known, was commissioned in August 1665 to transport 55 Quakers from Britain to the colonies as punishment for offences against the Conventicle Act which outlawed religious meetings other than those of the Church of England.

His departure was delayed and by October a third of the prisoners had died along with some of the crew thanks to the plague.

Then he was arrested for debt and the remaining crew mutinied. In February 1666 the ship finally set sail for the West Indies but she was seized by a Dutch privateer and the Quakers were freed.

He spun such a false tale of this adventure in his ship's logbook that his name entered the language as a word for a great lie, especially as told by a sailor.

Hobson's Choice

If you were in 17th century England and wanted to hire a horse you looked over the stable and selected your favourite beast. Unless you visited the livery stable of Thomas Hobson (1544-1631) in Cambridge which was rich with forty horses apparently available. However the truth was that you'd have no choice over which horse you got. All his customers got the horse nearest to the door.

The phrase now describes a position where there is no true choice available – the option is to take something, or nothing at all. An alternative phrase is "take it or leave it."

Hobson was an innkeeper. He ran the mail between London and Cambridge and rented out his horses to the students and staff of Cambridge University when not required for the mail coaches.

Although his phrase implies he was a miser, he gave generously to his city. He constructed Hobson's Conduit which brought clean drinking water to the city. His home is now owned by The National Trust and his inn still serves students of the city.

The poet John Milton knew Hobson and satirised him in several mock epitaphs.

Nosy Parker

A nosy (or nosey) parker is a person of an overly inquisitive or prying nature, someone with an excessive interest in the affairs of others.

The person most closely associated with the phrase is Anglican clergyman Matthew Parker (1504-1575). Parker was Archbishop of Canterbury from 1559 until his death.

As part of his work he ran several inquiries into the qualifications and activities of his clergy. His rather long nose could also have lent his name to the phrase.

Sadly he may be innocent of being the original nosy parker. The phrase first appeared in print in 1890 (three hundred years after his demise) and in the 17th century nosey just meant somebody with a large nose.

The phrase may have more to do with people sticking their nose in where it isn't required but there does appear to be some evidence that the archbishop was an early example, before the phrase was even coined.

Matthew Parker was a graduate of Cambridge and became chaplain to Anne Boleyn when she was queen, and later to Henry VIII. He survived the religious purges of Queen Mary's reign and was rewarded by Queen Elizabeth I by being made the first Archbishop of

Canterbury.

He married, happily, as soon as it was legal for Anglican clergy to do so but his queen disliked married clergy and insulted his wife. Parker survived very turbulent political and religious times and lived to a ripe age. Perhaps his interest in gossip enabled him to navigate those choppy waters.

Peeping Tom

A peeping tom is one who stares, typically at undressed women without their permission - an olde worlde stalker.

The original Tom, according to legend, was an English tailor who peeped at Lady Godiva. Lady Godiva was the kind wife of Leofric III, the 11th century Earl of Mercia and ruler of Coventry. She founded a monastery at Coventry in 1043 and there are many records of her charitable donations both solo and with her husband.

Godiva and his subjects begged King Leofric to reduce his high taxes. He said he would on the day she rode naked through the streets of the city without anybody looking at her. He presumably thought she wouldn't take this challenge or that she was so beautiful that all would gaze upon her.

His wife, Godiva, rose to his dare wearing nothing but her long hair. She asked the people to close their shutters and all did, except for the tailor. The story claims he was struck blind for his brazenness.

The story of Tom may be an embellishment (it only appears from the 18th century onwards) but historic land and tax records suggest Godiva's ride really happened. She is listed, by then a widow, in the Doomsday book, shortly after the Norman conquest of 1066 as one of the few Anglo-Saxon landowners and the only woman.

It is believed that her husband honoured his promise after her famous ride.

The Real McCoy

The real mccoy is the real deal, the genuine article. It is named for some great quality rum during the Prohibition years in the U.S.A..

Captain Bill McCoy was a rum-runner, smuggling in the finest quality rum for his clients in the Long Island area, possibly using a funeral parlour as a front for his dealings. You could trust him, and his goods, to be the real mccoy and the phrase came to indicate high quality produce of all types.

If only this were true. That McCoy is predated by a famous American boxer Ked "The Real" McCoy in the 1890s.

In the 1880s, however, McKays whiskey was exported from Scotland and cherished by Scottish emigrants in America who enjoyed a wee dram of the real McCoy or McKay as it was known back in their homeland.

Earlier again, c. 1860s, a prolific inventor called Elijah McCoy (1844-1929) made   products that were super reliable and popular. His work was copied but never equaled so consumers would seek out the real mccoy.

Elijah was born free in Canada to fugitive slave parents who had escaped using the famous Underground Railroad. He later became a U.S. citizen when the family returned there. He gained 57 patents during his lifetime, mainly relating to lubricating steam engines and is widely regarded as a pioneering African American engineer and inventor.

His products weren't sold under his name until the 1920s which may have prompted Captain McCoy to "borrow" the advertising slogan for his rum business. Elijah studied in Scotland early in his life and may have borrowed the phrase himself from the whiskey.

The identity of the original real McCoy is still open to

debate but lubrication, of one sort or another, is definitely involved.

Sweet Fanny Adams

This expression which means "nothing at all" dates to 1867 when an eight year old English girl called Fanny Adams (1859-1867) was found dismembered and mutilated. Her murderer, Frederick Baker, left pieces of her body in a field in Alton, Hampshire where her grave can be seen to this day. Baker, who was a solicitor's clerk, was convicted and hanged on Christmas Eve 1867.

At that time Royal Navy sailors were issued with canned mutton as a staple part of their diet. It was of poor quality and became known as sweet fanny adams because it was chopped up. Over time this transmuted to mean anything worthless or even "nothing at all".

The tins the mutton came in were often re-used as mess tins or cooking pots and these are still sometimes known as fannys.

Are Phrases a Good Way In?

The numerous phrases that appear to contain a person's name are nearly all disputed by language historians. Shank's mare didn't belong to a person called Shank. The peeping Tom was probably invented. Even Sophie and her choice were fictional.

Inserting your name into a phrase, and keeping it there in the face of urban myth and other claimants, may actually be harder than getting into the dictionary as a single word.

12
Unleash Your Inner Villain

We may not approve of villains but they certainly catch the public's imagination and as a result they have an easy route into the dictionary.

While serial killers like Jack the Ripper generate headlines they don't always enter the English dictionary. There are no guarantees and obviously I'm not promoting a life of crime.

Bobbitt

In 1993 Lorena Bobbitt (b. 1970) cut off the penis of John Wayne Bobbitt (b. 1967) with a kitchen knife while he was in a drunken sleep. Overnight their surname became a verb for castration.

Lorena was charged with malicious wounding but found not guilty by reason of insanity based on the long history of their abusive relationship. She threw the severed item from her car but it was found and re-attached.

The couple divorced after the court case and John went on to have a career in the adult entertainment industry under some terribly puntastic acting names. He later had more issues with the law.

Bowdlerise

To bowdlerise prose is a literary crime involving the removal of words and passages judged to be indecent.

The original bowdleriser was Thomas Bowdler (1734-1825), a British doctor and philanthropist. After he retired from medicine, he produced a "Family Shakespeare" with extensive help and editing by his sister Henrietta Marie Bowdler. Their edition cut and changed passages, characters and even plots so "those expressions are omitted which cannot with propriety be read aloud in a family". For example, Ophelia's suicide in "Hamlet" was changed to an accidental drowning. Inspired by its success he created a similarly expurgated version of Gibbon's "Decline and Fall of the Roman Empire" in 1823.

Bowdler's marriage to Elizabeth Trevennen was so unhappy his nephew, and his biographer, never even mentioned it in his life story. Although his name is now associated with unfair censorship of prose and other media, his family edition was reprinted five times in his lifetime, and many times thereafter, proving there was a market for such an edition of the Bard's works.

Bowdler is not the only person to have meddled with Shakespeare's works. Nahum Tate (1652-1715), Poet Laureate, rewrote "King Lear" to have a happy ending. Charles and Mary Lamb created children's editions of twenty of the plays, seldom quoting the original text.

Henrietta Bowdler (known as Harriet) was forced throughout her literary career to work anonymously or under her brother's name. Her novel "Pen Tamar, or the History of an Old Maid" was published after her death in 1830. Her sister Jane published a series of anonymous sermons which reached 50 editions that were so good a bishop offered the presumed clergyman author a parish in his diocese.

Machiavellian

Machiavellian is an adjective generally used to describe that rare beast, a devious and scheming politician.

Niccolò di Bernardo dei Machiavelli (1469-1527) was an Italian Renaissance historian, diplomat, politician, writer, and philosopher who is sometimes credited as the founder of political science.

When the Medici family gained power in Florence in 1512 Machiavelli lost his high-ranking government job. Then he was imprisoned and tortured for conspiring against them.

He wrote comedies, songs, poetry, and most famously "The Prince" in 1513 (which wasn't published until 1532, after his death). This short book outlined methods for a ruler to maintain their power, regardless of ethics and morals. When published it was vilified as evil both for this and his humanist comparing of Christ to other pagan gods on equal footing. His central tenet was a ruler is better to be greatly feared rather than greatly loved by his people. The book was banned by the Catholic church.

More recent commentators on the book suggest it was entirely ironic or that it was destined for the common people's enlightenment. The ruling classes already knew the oppressive lessons contained in his book.

Masochism

Masochism is the mental disorder which causes a person to derive pleasure, particularly of a sexual nature, from experiencing self-inflicted pain and humiliation.

It is named for the writings of Austrian author Leopold von Sacher-Masoch (1836-1895) which depict this condition, in particular his novel "Venus in Furs" about a man whose chief pleasure in life was to be thrashed by a beautiful lady clad only in a fur coat.

Leopold didn't just include masochism in his writings. During his lifetime he was the slave of several mistresses and two wives.

He had an unusual upbringing. His father was chief of police of the city of Lviv in the Ukraine at a time of uprising and he concocted a scheme to pay peasants who brought in the heads of noblemen. Yes, their heads. His son Leopold wasn't impressed.

Leopold was a well-known author of romantic short fiction, folk tales, and historic fiction in his day and travelled widely but sadly ended his days in an insane asylum.

Leopold is Marianne Faithfull's great-great uncle on her mother's side.

Ponzi

Charles Ponzi (1882-1949) was the Italian conman, born Carlo Ponzi, who in 1920s America worked a swindle on international postal reply coupons where he gave huge profits to early investors by using the investments of later suckers to pay them. It ran for over a year before collapse and cost his investors over 20 million dollars (over 250 million in today's terms). He didn't invent the trick but it became associated with his name.

He served about ten years in prison as a result of this con trick but while there received Christmas cards and requests for more investments from his previous customers.

In his last interview, before his death in a charity hospital in Rio, Ponzi who was now blind and partially paralysed said the scheme was "cheap at that price" and that it was the best show in America. "It was easily worth fifteen million bucks to watch me put the thing over."

Quisling

A quisling is a traitor who collaborates with an invading enemy.

Vidkun Abraham Quisling (1887-1945) was a Norwegian army officer and politician who worked with the Germans during WWII. He served in the Norwegian army and later in the diplomatic service in Russia and the League of Nations.

In 1933 Quisling formed the fascist National Union party but never gained a seat in parliament. In 1939 he urged German occupation of Norway. When Hitler invaded Norway in April 1940 Quisling became a puppet Minister President.

Under his rule a thousand Jews were sent to concentration camps. He lived in a reinforced 46-room villa on an island near Oslo and had food tasters in case of poisoning attempts on his life.

He was arrested when the Germans surrendered Oslo in May 1945, found guilty of embezzlement, murder, and high treason. He was shot by firing squad in October

1945. His former home is now a Holocaust museum.

Sadist

A sadist is one who derives pleasure from inflicting pain on others.

Sadism is named for the French soldier, aristocrat, revolutionary, and writer Count Donatien Alphonse François de Sade (1740-1814) who was known as the Marquis de Sade.

His many writings included novels, plays, short fiction, and political tracts but the works that gained him an entry in the dictionary were erotic works depicting sexual perversions. He combined philosophical discourse arguing for extreme freedoms with pornography with an emphasis on violence and blasphemy against the Catholic church. He was the first author to discuss abortion for population control.

He used his position as employer to molest and assault many servants, both male and female, but later met Marie-Constance Quesnet, a former actress and spent the remaining 24 years of his life with her.

His most famous books were written while he was imprisoned for sexual offences.

He was transferred from the Bastille just days before its famous storming on the 14th of July 1789.

De Sade was elected a delegate to the National Convention during the French Revolution.

His final years were spent in a mental asylum in Charenton. He was behind bars for 32 years of his life. He was imprisoned by Napoleon in 1801 because of his writings.

His skull was removed from his grave for phrenological examination – the pseudo-science of reading a man's character from the bumps on his head.

For many years his descendants suppressed their links to the infamous marquis but since the 1940s they've been re-claiming their ancestor and publishing his lesser-known works.

Being a Villain for the Dictionary

It is doubtful if becoming an infamous villain is worth it to enter the English language. It's hard to ignore the fact that most of the entries in this chapter ended their days alone, poverty-stricken, imprisoned, or executed. Would a dictionary entry compensate for that?

However, eponymous villains are tough to ignore.

13
The Scientific Way

Scientific inventions have already been covered, but there are two more ways that science could edge you into the English language and in one case it's not what you do, but who you know.

Discoveries in science, and geography, often result in naming rights. Identify a new element and generally speaking you get some input on its name. The same goes for a star, a unit of measurement, a mountain range, disease, or obscure beetle. I can't include all of these without turning this book into a multi-volume work. Plus obscure beetles rarely become part of common everyday English, but I am providing a selection of units of measurement.

A surprisingly number of scientific discoveries are *not* named for their discoverer. Some scientists honoured patrons, colleagues, and inspirational figures rather than claiming all the fame for themselves. Perhaps the easiest scientific route to the dictionary is befriending a scientist.

Amp

Amp, the unit of electrical current, is actually short for ampere and it is named for the French physicist André Marie Ampère (1775-1836) who was noted for his discoveries on electricity and magnetism. However he did not devise the amp as a unit.

He proposed the existence of the electron, discovered the element fluorine, and grouped elements by their properties 50 years before the periodic table we now know.

Largely self-educated, Ampère buried himself in his work after two tragic incidents in his personal life. When he was 18 he witnessed his father's guillotining during the Reign of Terror. He didn't speak for an entire year thereafter. He married when he was 24, but his wife died just one year later.

He hosted the young Frédéric Ozanam in his home for a time. Ozanam went on to found the Society of Saint Vincent de Paul.

Ampère's name is inscribed on the Eiffel Tower along with 71 other famous engineers and scientists.

Curie

The curie is a unit of radioactivity and it is named for Marie Sklodowska Curie (1867-1934).

Curie was the first woman to win a Nobel Prize, the first and only woman to win twice, and the only person to win it in two different sciences (physics in 1903 and chemistry in 1911). Only 5% of all Nobel Prizes awarded to date have been to women, with two of them in physics. She won her prize for physics jointly with her husband and Henri Becquerel. The committee originally intended to award it only to the two male scientists but one member told Pierre and he insisted his wife be recognised too.

She coined the term radioactivity, developed techniques to isolate radioactive isotopes, and discovered two elements – polonium and radium. She created and ran x-ray units in field hospitals in World War I. Her husband Pierre, also a scientist, dropped his own research on crystals to join her research which they conducted in a leaky shed on university grounds. They did not patent their discoveries which proved to be very valuable to industry.

Pierre died in 1906 in a traffic accident. Marie continued their work, becoming the first female professor at the University of Paris. She died many years later due to exposure to radium during her research and to x-rays during her field hospital work.

Curie studied at the clandestine flying university in Warsaw before working to fund her studies in Paris. The flying university was an educational establishment that didn't agree with ruling policy at the time and had to meet in secret. They admitted female students and allowed the use of laboratory equipment which had been banned in schools following uprisings.

Curie's papers, and even her cookbook, from the 1890s are so highly contaminated by radioactivity that they are stored in lead boxes and require specialist clothing to be viewed.

Decibel

{thanks to Dianne Thomas at www.diannethomas.net }

A decibel is the unit of sound (actually one tenth of a "bel") and is named for Alexander Graham Bell (1847-1922) the Scottish scientist who co-invented the telephone.

Both his mother and his wife were deaf. His father, grandfather, and brother all worked in the area of speech for the deaf. Alexander was partly homeschooled and showed promise from a young age at problem solving in particular. He was creating working, useful inventions from the age of 12.

He moved to Canada with his family at the age of 23 for the sake of his health and later to Boston. He worked with Thomas Watson on the design and patent of the first practical telephone. Watson was able to implement Bell's ideas. In 1876 Bell made the first phone call saying "Watson, come here, I want you."

Bell felt the correct way to answer a phone call was "ahoy" and always answered the phone in that manner. Thomas Edison preferred "hello" and it's the standard answer to this day.

Bell experimented widely across sciences and in many cases touched on topics that are surprisingly contemporary. He pressed a magnetic field on a record – something which later was used for tape recording and floppy disc storage.

He created a composting toilet and speculated that solar panels could heat the houses of the future. He also predicted phones with video capability. He worried about peak oil and predicted a greenhouse effect due to burning fossil fuels. He worked on early flight experiments and hydrofoils.

Less honourably he was interested in eugenics and promoted the sterilisation of people who carried defective genes for the human race. By the late 1930s half the states in the U.S. had laws along these lines which were used as a basis for those enacted in Nazi Germany.

In January 1915 he was invited to make the first transcontinental phone call. He rang Watson.

When he died, the entire phone system was shut for one minute in his honour.

Faraday or Farad

A farad is a unit of charge of one mole of electrons. Although this isn't a commonly used English term it would be unfair to exclude Michael Faraday from a list featuring amps, watts, and volts.

Michael Faraday (1791-1867) was born to a poor London family. He was apprenticed to a bookbinder at the age of 14 and became intrigued by the scientific books he was binding. He educated himself over the next seven years. He started going to Royal Institution lectures, persuaded Humphry Davy (see Davy lamps above) to take him on as a valet/lab assistant after he saw him lecture, and thus started the career of one of the most important physicists.

Initially Faraday worked at the Royal Institution preparing experiments for eminent scientists of the day and in 1826 founded the Friday Evening Discourses, and the Christmas Lectures which continue to this day (and are televised on the BBC). He gave many of the lectures himself and delighted in colourful experiments to illustrate his discoveries.

In 1831 he discovered electromagnetic induction (the principle behind generators and transformers) which moved electricity from a curiosity into a new technology with practical uses. He coined words like cathode, ion, and electrode. He also discovered electrolysis.

In an era when science was largely the preserve of wealthy noblemen he was never entirely accepted as part of the elite. He was offered a knighthood in recognition of his services to science but he turned it down on religious grounds. When asked to consult on the use of chemical weapons in the Crimean War (1853-1856) he also refused. His portrait featured on the British pound note from 1991 to 2001.

Albert Einstein kept a picture of Faraday on his wall, along with Isaac Newton.

Volt

The volt is the metric unit of electric potential. It is named for Italian physicist Count Alessandro Volta (1745-1827).

Volta is noted for inventing the first true battery, the voltaic cell, in 1800. He isolated methane for the first time and discovered it could be ignited with a spark when mixed with air. This is the basis of the internal combustion engine which powers most cars.

Volta didn't speak until he was four but thereafter proved an able student, learning to speak his native Italian plus Latin, French, English, and German.

His discovery of the first battery was unintentional. His experiments were performed to disprove the claims of Luigi Galvani (see galvanise, Inventions chapter) about animal electricity being similar to static electricity.

Volta realised Galvani's frogs' legs were moving due to the contact with different metals rather than contact with the dead frogs.

The battery unleashed a surge of innovation. Within weeks scientists had used it to break water into hydrogen and oxygen. Within a few years Humphry Davy (davy lamp, see above) used it to discover seven new elements.

Widely praised in his lifetime, Volta won many awards and medals. His friend Napoleon made him a count in 1801.

Watt

The metric unit of power is called a watt after the Scottish engineer and inventor James Watt (1736-1819).

He worked in Glasgow University as an instrument repairer and when maintaining the 1712 Newcomen steam engine there in 1765 he realised it could be improved with the addition of a condenser and could be adapted to do more than just pump water. His new Watt engine soon replaced the Newcomen and kick-started the industrial revolution and age of steam.

He worked in partnership with Matthew Boulton, a businessman and engineer, to make steam engines and became a wealthy man. Together they coined the term horsepower and the partners appeared on the 2011 British £50 pound note.

Watt is also known for inventing a centrifugal governor and a manuscript copying machine which was used in offices into the 1900s.

Although a popular man in scientific circles throughout his life, he struggled with the business side of his inventions. He claimed "he would rather face a loaded cannon than settle an account or make a bargain".

His attic workshop is now on display in London's Science Museum.

The Scientific Way In

Entering the dictionary is far from easy and having a scientific unit named in your honour is equally difficult as the lives of these scientists prove. Their contributions to modern life are indisputable. If you can match them then you've earned your dictionary entry and nobody will quibble.

14
Salmagundi

Salmagundi is not an eponym, sadly, as being introduced to Ms. Salmagundi at a dinner party would be a real conversation-starter. Salmagundi is a mish-mash of a dish dating from the 1600s which was never exactly the same any time it was made. The chef could include anything – meat, fish, edible flowers, eggs, fruit, nuts. These cold ingredients, whatever you had available, would be topped with a spicy dressing and your dish was complete. Apparently pirates loved it.

To complete the dish of eponyms I can't resist certain entries which simply don't fit in the other chapters. These ones don't have a connecting theme but deserve a place in any eponym list. Welcome to the eponym salmagundi.

Annie Oakley

Annie Oakley is American theatre slang for a free ticket.

Phoebe Ann Oakley Mosey Butler (1860-1926) was the star rifle-shooter in Buffalo Bill's "Wild West Show". Her most-renowned trick was to toss a five of hearts playing card into the air and then shoot a hole through each pip on the card. The free theatre tickets have a hole punched in them (to prevent re-sale) which reminded audiences of her prowess.

By the age of 15 she'd earned so much hunting game for a grocery store that she paid off the mortgage on her mother's home. The Native-American leader Sitting Bull gave her the name "Little Sure Shot". When she performed for Kaiser Wilhelm II she shot a cigarette out of his mouth.

During the Spanish-American War (and World War I) she volunteered to organise a regiment of female sharp-shooters but was refused. Instead she raised funds for the Red Cross with exhibition shows. She taught about 15,000 women how to shoot during her lifetime as she felt it was a vital skill. Although a vocal campaigner for female participation in business and military life she couldn't bring herself to support votes for women saying it was acceptable "if only the good women voted".

Her husband, also a sharp-shooter, died three weeks after her. She spent her entire fortune on her family and her charity work.

Buckminsterfullerene

{with thanks to Rosemary Costello}

Buckminsterfullerne, an allotrope of carbon, was discovered in 1985 and earned the discoverers the Nobel Prize in 1996. It is roughly soccer-ball shaped. It was named after Buckminster Fuller who was famous for designing geodesic domes which have a similar structure. These and other fullerenes are known as buckyballs in his honour. Fullerenes are used as catalysts, lubricants, in nanotubes to strengthen materials, and in drug delivery systems.

Richard Buckminster "Bucky" Fuller (1895-1983) was an American architect, designer, inventor, and author.

Although he objected to the label "inventor" later in his life, by the age of twelve he'd created a device, using an umbrella, to allow the person rowing a boat to face in the direction of travel.

He attended Harvard and was expelled twice, once for partying hard with a vaudeville troupe. He worked in various jobs, served in the U.S. navy in World War I, and ran a business with his father-in-law which failed.

By 1927 he was the parent of one child and totally broke. He re-assessed his life, possibly with a spiritual revelation to guide him, and began to focus on helping humanity to do more with less. He wanted to design inexpensive shelter and transport options.

He designed dymaxion houses and cars (three prototypes of these flying cars were built during the Great Depression) and popularised the geodesic dome – examples include the Montreal Biosphere and the Eden Project in the U.K.. He also designed a floating city and promoted sustainable design.

He travelled so much for his work that he wore three wristwatches for the various time-zones. He coined and changed many commonly used words to better express his vision for the world but probably the only one that stuck was "Spaceship Earth".

Buckminster was president of Mensa from 1974-1983. He and his wife died within two days of each other.

Casanova

A casanova is a womaniser noted for his romantic adventures, typically with many partners. The term comes from Italian adventurer and author Giovanni Jacopo Casanova (1725-1798) whose biography reads like a work of fiction.

He was born in Venice, the son of an actor and actress. He was expelled at the age of 16 from a seminary for monks for his immoral behaviour and later, something of a dandy already, studied at the University of Padua and graduated with a degree in law. He took "minor orders" to become a monk while still a student and an inveterate gambler.

His first patron, an elderly Venetian senator, taught him about food, wine, and how to behave in society but drove him out when he discovered Casanova had already seduced the actress he had his eye on.

His second patron, a cardinal, set him to writing love letters on his behalf and introduced him to the Pope before dismissing him for scandal.

He joined the army but by the age of 21 he had abandoned that career for professional gambling and then work as a violinist. This didn't last long. He saved the life of a nobleman, thus acquiring his third patron until a prank of his involving a fresh corpse went badly wrong and he had to flee the city.

He went on to live in many European cities, making and losing friends and money along the way. He worked as a preacher, philosopher, diplomat, gambler, spy, violinist, and broke hearts everywhere. He wrote plays and other works including science fiction. He met many of the celebrities of the day – Catherine the Great, King George III of England, Benjamin Franklin, Madame de Pompadour, Rousseau, Mozart, Voltaire, and Goethe.

His romantic dalliances were like the plot of an opera. He once escaped prison in the Doge's palace by digging his way out of the roof with a priest, climbing down a bed sheet rope, and convincing a guard they'd been locked in by mistake at the end of a function.

He finally settled down in his fifties as a librarian to Count von Waldstein in Bohemia and wrote his twelve volume memoirs which were published 1826-1838.

Douglas Fir

This very tall American evergreen tree is named for the Scottish botanist and great plant-hunter David Douglas (1798-1834).

Douglas learned his trade as a gardener at Scone Palace, later studying at Glasgow University. The Royal Horticultural Society sent him to North America at the age of 23 on a plant-hunting trip. On three trips Douglas crossed Canada on foot and travelled as far south as California.

When he came across these tall trees, second only to giant sequoias and redwoods, he shot down the seeds with a gun and was chased by Native Americans. He collected over 200 plants and seeds not known in Europe such as sitka spruce, lupin, penstemon, and California poppies. Over 80 species of plants have douglasii in their Latin names in his honour.

When he was 35 and working in Hawaii he fe l into a hunting pit and was crushed by a wild bull which also fell in. A small stand of douglas fir trees now marks the location of his death.

Jeremiad

A jeremiad is a rant, tirade, or diatribe and is generally written down. It may predict the downfall of current society due to its flaws.

The first known use of jeremiad was in 1780 and it

comes from French via Latin from the prophet Jeremiah (c. 626-587 B.C.). He features in the Book of Jeremiah, the Book of Kings, and the Book of Lamentations in the Old Testament. He is best known for predicting the downfall of the Kingdom of Judah and is sometimes known as the weeping prophet.

His prophecies did not give him a happy life. He was imprisoned and had to flee for his life to Egypt. Historians can't confirm Jeremiah existed outside of the Bible's pages.

Jeremiad was a popular name choice with early Puritan settlers in North America.

John Doe

A John Doe is an unknown male. Jane Doe is the female equivalent.

John Doe is commonly mentioned in TV detective shows but his history is more ancient that you might expect. John Doe and Richard Roe were the names given to two parties in legal documents since the 1300s and may even date back to the Magna Carta in 1215. The names were used when witnesses didn't give their names or didn't want their names recorded. John Doe was the plaintiff and Richard Roe was the defendant. Probably the most famous legal use of Roe is in the landmark U.S. Supreme Court case Roe v. Wade.

By the 1800s the name John Doe had become an everyman in common usage. From there it moved to describe an unknown person in legal/police use – an unknown suspect (or un-sub), or a body whose identity is yet to be found. In the U.K. the name Joe Bloggs is more common as a placeholder name of this variety.

It is unlikely that there was an original John Doe in history as the name was chosen deliberately to obscure true identities.

Jumbo

This adjective is used to mean large and is part of the airplane name jumbo jet.

Jumbo (1861-1885) was the name of a 62 ton African elephant captured in the Sudan and exhibited in London Zoo from 1865 to 1882.

Despite an outcry, including a protest from Queen Victoria and 100,000 school children, Jumbo was bought by PT Barnum, the famous American showman in 1882. Jumbo was then exhibited in "Barnum and Bailey's

Greatest Show on Earth". During his three and a half years in the show it is estimated that he carried a million children on his back.

He was fond of Scottish whiskey.

Jumbo died in 1885 when a train hit him while he was trying to rescue Tom Thumb, Barnum's smallest elephant. The animals were being herded across the tracks to their own train. Tom Thumb survived, the oncoming train de-railed, and Jumbo died, with his trunk curled around his trainer. This version of his death, created by the great showman himself, may be partially untrue, you decide.

Jumbo was either named from the phrase mumbo-jumbo (meaning nonsense) or from jumbe (the Swahili word for chief), or from jambo (meaning hello).

Jumbo's skeleton was donated to the American Museum of Natural History in New York.

Malapropisms

The use of a similarly sounding but incorrect word in a phrase or sentence is a malapropism. An example would be Constable Dogberry in "Much Ado about Nothing" telling Governor Leonato "Our watch, sir, have indeed comprehended two auspicious persons" when he really meant they had apprehended two suspicious persons.

Malapropisms aren't limited to fiction but they are named after a fictional character, Mrs. Malaprop in the 1775 play "The Rivals" by Irish playwright Richard Brinsley Sheridan (1751-1816) because her lines are littered with them. Sheridan wasn't the originator of such utterances as clearly Shakespeare got there first. Laurel and Hardy also used them, as did Ronnie Barker.

Politicians are tripped up by malapropisms regularly, perhaps because their public utterances are scrutinised by the press. Bertie Ahern, former Taoiseach of Ireland, warned the country against upsetting the apple tart (cart) of economic success. Richard J. Daley, former Chicago Mayor called a tandem bicycle a tantrum bicycle.

"The Rivals" was George Washington's favourite play.

Sheridan wrote the play in a hurry to clear debts after his youthful elopement. It had to be completely revised after a disastrous opening night (the audience threw fruit at the cast) but it went on to huge success. Sheridan became a theatre-owner, famous comic playwright, and later a member of parliament noted for his witty remarks during debates.

Maverick

A maverick is an independent person who doesn't wish to conform.

American pioneer Samuel Augustus Maverick (1803-1870) became a rancher when he received a herd of cattle as payment of a debt. He failed to brand all his calves. He was more interested in his land than the livestock and unbranded cattle became known as mavericks. This transferred to mean anybody who didn't bear the brand of another, a free thinker, someone who wouldn't go with the herd.

He claimed he didn't want to brand them as it was painful. Other ranchers believed he wanted to collect any other unbranded cattle for himself. He sold the herd after eleven years and never held livestock again.

Samuel lived a varied life. He graduated from Yale and became a lawyer but he also ran a goldmine and a plantation. He was a rancher in Texas before fighting for Texan independence from Mexico. He narrowly avoided being caught up in the Battle of the Alamo, having left to seek reinforcements before the final battle. He also served as mayor of San Antonio.

He narrowly escaped death three times – once at the Alamo, once on a land surveying trip when his camp was slaughtered the day after he left early, and once when his boat capsized and he lost all his land deeds.

Samuel served as a congressman in the Texas legislature. His grandson, Fontaine Maury Maverick, became a congressman and coined the word gobbledygook in frustration over red tape delays.

Poinsettia

{with thanks to Nell Jenda}

Poinsettia is a plant in the spurge family with red and green foliage that is popular at Christmas time. It is named for Joel Roberts Poinsett (1779-1851), an American politician and diplomat.

Joel was born to a wealthy South Carolina family and travelled extensively in Europe as a young man. His father died while he was away and he became the sole heir to a large fortune which enabled even more travels around Russia and Arabia where he gained introductions to many local rulers.

After his return home he served as a U.S. diplomat to Chile and Argentina. He won a place in the U.S. House of

Representatives in 1820 but shortly afterwards resigned to serve as the first U.S. ambassador to Mexico. It was while travelling there that Joel, an amateur botanist, found the plant that now bears his name.

After Mexico he served as Secretary of War for four years. Thereafter he worked towards establishing a national museum. His efforts ultimately led to the founding of the Smithsonian.

Sequoia

The sequoia is the most massive tree in the world and is named for Sequoyah (c. 1770-1843).

Sequoyah (the h is optional) was a Cherokee silversmith who believed himself to be the son of a white trader and adopted the name George Guess. He became lame early in life, possibly thanks to a hunting accident. He lived with his mother who ran a trading post. Unable to farm or be a warrior he turned to making jewellery and after his mother's death, ran her trading post and became a self-taught, and successful, blacksmith.

He dealt regularly with the local settlers and was impressed with their writing. He called letters "talking leaves" and was convinced the source of the white man's power was in the written language.

He set about creating a 86 character alphabet for the Cherokee language despite the mockery of his friends and family. Most Cherokee believed writing was either sorcery or pretence.

It took him twelve years to create. He completed it in 1821. He taught it first to his six year old daughter as adults were unwilling. He travelled with her to various Cherokee reserves to demonstrate the syllabary with her help. Within a few years the Cherokee had a higher literacy rate than surrounding European-American settlers.

Seven years after he finished the syllabary, Cherokee printed the first ever Cherokee and English language newspaper, "The Cherokee Phoenix". The news of his work spread around the world and inspired the creation of 21 new scripts for over 65 languages from China to Liberia and Alaska.

Sequoyah later worked on creating something similar for use amongst all Native American tribes. He dedicated much of his later life to reuniting the splintered portions of the Cherokee Nation and died on a journey for that purpose.

Spoonerism

Reverend William Archibald Spooner (1844-1930) was renowned for slips of the tongue in which the initial sounds in words were transposed with comic effect. He has given his name to such mistakes, be they deliberate or accidental.

The Oxford cleric would extoll the virtues of a "well-boiled icicle" when he meant a well-oiled bicycle. He described God as a "shoving leopard" instead of a loving shepherd. He called Queen Victoria "our queer old dean" rather than a dear old queen.

The term spoonerism was well-established in the English language during his lifetime which probably added extra pressure whenever he had to preach.

It is likely that the clergyman's verbal mistakes were due to his extremely poor eyesight.

Spooner was known as a genial and kindly man during his 60 years at New College, Oxford. He was notably absent-minded in other areas during his life. Once he invited a don to tea to welcome a new fellow of the college called Stanley Casson. Unfortunately he was speaking to Stanley himself.

Tuckerisation

The use of a real person's name for a fictional character in a story as an in-joke is called tuckerisation after Wilson Tucker (1914-2006), a pioneering science fiction writer.

Generally this trick is used for minor characters only. Philip K. Dick tuckerised his fellow author Poul Anderson in his story "Waterspider" by sending him to a future where sci-fi authors were seen as having precognitive abilities.

Tuckerisations are sometimes auctioned off to fans for charity fundraising.

Tucker became involved in science fiction initially as a fan. He published fanzines from 1932 to 2001 and was involved in many fan conventions too. He coined many phrases in the genre, such as "space opera". He won Hugo awards for fan writing and fanzines. His own novels and short fiction were well received too and he wrote humour pieces under the pseudonym Hoy Ping Pong.

The Salmagundi Method

If nothing else, this salmagundi of eponyms proves there are more ways into the dictionary than could ever be contained in one book. People are remarkably various. Their lives take twists that would never be credible in fiction. Those experiences catch the imagination in surprising ways and a new English word is born.

Conclusion

The English language changes constantly. Words enter from ancient languages. Words change meaning with use and abuse. We use the language daily, changing t to suit our needs. It flexes and expands to cope. Dictionaries are re-printed annually for a good reason.

The extraordinary people in this book who gave their names to English will be joined by others tomorrow. Some will be temporary additions, others will last. Many of the entries in my selection are thousands of years old and their lives are still inspirational. If you want a place in history, become an eponym.

More importantly, if you want to be an eponym, live an interesting life. Challenge the world to change. Explore, invent, create.

Getting into the dictionary isn't an easy process but striving for the extraordinary is a good start.

Thanks

Every week since 2009 I've played with unusual words on the Wordfoolery blog (https://wordfoolery.wordpress.com). A wonderful community of readers enrich the blog with word suggestions and their passion for language. Without them this book wouldn't exist.

A number of friends and fellow wordfools suggested eponyms for inclusion in this book, you will see their names beside the words they suggested. Many thanks to Nell Jenda, Rick Ellrod, Peter Sheehan, Diane Thomas, and Rosemary Costello. Thanks also to Noelle and Paddy for endless cake and encouragement.

Sheena McDonald did an amazing job of proof-reading and I love Peter Sheehan's cover design.

Every November for the last ten years I've taken part in NaNoWriMo (National Novel Writing Month), as a writer and mentor to the Ireland NorthEast region which is filled with amazing writers of all ages and genres. 2016 was my first non-fiction NaNoWriMo and it enabled me to draft the first version of the book you're now reading.

If you've ever thought of writing a book, I urge you to try NaNoWriMo at www.nanowrimo.org. You get a whole thirty days to write 50,000 words.

Finally I offer my love and thanks to Brendan, Daniel, and Eleanor. They tolerate my disappearing to write and inspire me more than they will ever know. I hope they enjoy the book and will stop greeting my wordy trivia with "I bet that's an eponym" coupled with a long sigh.

Further Reading

Eponyms abound in the English language but a good starting list can be found in Martin Manser's "Dictionary of Eponyms" (pub Sphere, 1988).

A perfect starting point for biographical information on the people behind the eponyms is always Wikipedia and I also heartily recommend the trivia-filled Breverton books. "Breverton's Nautical Curiosities" by Terry Breverton, Quercus 2010 was particularly helpful this time.

I used many sources and my own previous experience in writing and computing to create this book, but I am happy to recommend "APE: Author, Publisher, Entrepreneur – How to Publish a Book" by Guy Kawasaki and Shawn Welch as a good starting point for those interested in becoming indie publishers. It was easily the best overview I found as well as being admirably up to date with technical details.

About the Author

Grace Tierney (www.gracetierney.com) is a columnist, author, and blogger writing in rural Ireland. She is the Ireland North East organiser for National Novel Writing Month (www.NaNoWriMo.org) and actually enjoys the challenge of writing 50,000 words in one month. She blogs about unusual words at http://wordfoolery.wordpress.com, tweets @Wordfoolery, and serialises contemporary comic fiction at www.channillo.com.

Her favourite eponymous hero is Casanova because his life was so extraordinary, definitely not the average librarian.

www.facebook.com/gracetierneywriter - writing / life

www.instagram.com/wordfoolery/ – history via photos

www.pinterest.co.uk/GraceTierneyIrl/ - crafts, writing, history

If You Enjoyed This Book

Grace blogs every week about the history of unusual words on Wordfoolery (http://wordfoolery.wordpress.com). Drop by, all word-lovers are welcome. She takes requests so if you have a favourite obscure word, suggest it. Upcoming books inspired by the blog include "Words the Sea Gave Us", "Words the Vikings Gave Us", "Words the Greeks Gave Us", etc.

The easiest and cost-free way to thank an author of any book, but especially one who wears the indie-publisher hat, is to post an honest review. It makes a huge difference to the visibility of the book and future sales, so if you enjoyed this romp through the history of eponyms, please take a couple of minutes to review it. Thank you so much.

Index